ArtMaking

Other Redleaf Press Books by Michelle Kay Compton and Robin Chappele Thompson

StoryMaking: The Maker Movement Approach to Literacy for Early Learners
Makerspaces: Remaking Your Play and STEAM Early Learning Areas
StoryMakers on Deck: StoryMaking Provocations with Children

ArtMaking

Using Picture Books and Art to Read Our World

Michelle Kay Compton, MA

and Robin Chappele Thompson, PhD

Redleaf Press®
www.redleafpress.org
800-423-8309

Published by Redleaf Press
10 Yorkton Court
St. Paul, MN 55117
www.redleafpress.org

First edition 2022
Cover design by Danielle Carnito
Interior design by Percolator Graphic Design
Typeset in Elena
Printed in the United States of America
29 28 27 26 25 24 23 22   1 2 3 4 5 6 7 8

Library of Congress Cataloging-in-Publication Data

Names: Compton, Michelle Kay, author. | Thompson, Robin, 1960– author.
Title: ArtMaking : using picture books and art to read our world / by Michelle Kay Compton, MA, and Robin Chappele Thompson, PhD.
Description: First edition. | St. Paul, MN : Redleaf Press, 2022. | Includes bibliographical references. | Summary: "In this book, children are invited to 'read their worlds' as they learn about images, explore materials and elements of art (color, lines, shapes, textures, spaces, design) and communicate their thinking through their own art processes and products. Using artwork as well as illustrations from children's books as provocations, children make meaning with their visual literacy skills as they use the receptive and productive languages of literacy and art to make connections"— Provided by publisher.
Identifiers: LCCN 2021059938 (print) | LCCN 2021059939 (ebook) | ISBN 9781605547633 (paperback) | ISBN 9781605547640 (ebook)
Subjects: LCSH: Art—Study and teaching (Early childhood) | Art in education.
Classification: LCC LB1139.5.A78 C66 2022 (print) | LCC LB1139.5.A78 (ebook) | DDC 372.5/044—dc23/eng/20220106
LC record available at https://lccn.loc.gov/2021059938
LC ebook record available at https://lccn.loc.gov/2021059939

Printed on acid-free paper

Contents

Acknowledgments

Michelle

Robin, thank you for challenging and inspiring me to think about art in new and innovative ways. I have always been intimidated to see and understand art. With your guidance and encouragement, you have given me the gift of "reading our world" in new ways. I am proud of how we played alongside children to discover this ArtMaking process so children can make meaning with books and express themselves using the mentor artists you introduced to me. I am forever grateful for our friendship, your enthusiasm for learning, and the constant support of your family, who thankfully give us advice and help for free.

To my ESK family: Dr. Talmadge and Beth Sterchi, thank you for inviting me to join the incredible team of educators at ESK! You have created a culture where you celebrate and cheer on your staff, welcome and create meaningful connections with your families, and cultivate fun and enriching experiences for your children. Thank you for your constant support to help me achieve my ideas and dreams through your encouragement and for searching out ways to help me fulfill my ongoing "wish list." Anna Calhoun, thank you for always allowing me to brainstorm ideas with you and teaching me about artists. You are a talented and knowledgeable art teacher and ArtMaker, and I am thankful to work with you. Anna Ottaviano, thank you for bringing light, laughter, and deep meaning to our teaching each day. To all of you in the ESK family, I'm blessed to be able to learn from each one of you each day!

To my family, thank you for continuing to believe in my passion for researching and teaching and for cheering me along the way. I am beyond thankful for the support of my husband, Shawn, who helps me accomplish my dreams, who equally parents our boys, and who ensures that our needs come before his own. My two very energetic boys, Cole and Cai, continually inspire me. Boys, thank you for inviting me into your worlds of play and showing me the power of your ideas and art. You are ArtMakers and have helped me become a confident one too!

Robin

As always and forever, thank you to Michelle, the best partner, mama, colleague, teacher, encourager, ArtMaker. I'm forever thankful our paths crossed and I get to call you my friend.

I'm also forever grateful for my wonderful team and friends in the Manatee County School District. Jodi O'Meara (amazing author and expert on differentiating instruction, with a special love for children with special rights), Luanne Howe (the most optimistic and positive force, inspires with knowledge, kindness, and rainbow hair), and Angela Knapek (amazing teacher of teachers, fellow gardener, lover of dogs and children) are the most amazing early learning specialists, friends, colleagues, and ArtMakers, always willing to go the extra mile for the benefit of children. Thank you for your willingness to "try out" ideas, projects, learning engagements, mediums, loose parts, books, and more. Thank you for making me laugh, keeping me thinking, raising hard questions, and always providing insights about how and what children learn during

ArtMaking. I feel like I'm the luckiest person in the world, getting to work with you each day. You fill my days with joy. Thank you.

I owe a debt of gratitude to some fantastic prekindergarten teachers, always open to trying new ideas. Lynne Gangarosa (most beautiful and inspirational provocations, lover of children's books); Michelle Garcia-Vasquez (never afraid of the mess and always willing to try something new); Charlotte (April) Sylvain (her children never ceased to amaze us with their visual literacy discoveries); Emily Taylor (working with her families, laying out beautiful plans, and delighting in her children's accomplishments); and partners Bea Schaeffer (a "real" art teacher who offered new perspectives and ideas) and Marie Mannion and Lauri Halm (also "real" art teachers in their amazing pre-K ArtMaking classrooms). These ArtMakers are doing the hard work to ensure our children are successful readers, writers, makers, artists . . . ArtMakers. Thank you.

My family members continue to amaze me with their intellect, compassion, empathy, support, adventuresome spirit, beauty, love of life, and willingness to do anything that might make my life better at any given moment. My two amazing daughters (Dacie and Glori), the two best sons-in-law (Dennis and Will), the sweetest grandson (Thatcher), a mom (Charlotte) who is my biggest fan, and a husband (Wade) who somehow made all things possible. Thankful beyond words.

"Look at all the lines dancing across the page! Lines can make beautiful pictures, and we can too!" the children shouted. As Ann Pelo writes, "Art can be a way of thinking, feeling, imagining, relating, and expressing. Art can be a way to be in the world" (2017, 1). And what a wonderful way to be in the world!

Introduction

Making Meaning
with ArtMaking

It was three months into ArtMaking when Bowman rushed into the classroom to share a book he had discovered. "Look at all the lines in the pictures! Can I show everyone for ArtMaking today?" For the next week, the children pored over the illustrations, noticing the colors and lines and retelling events. They inferred meaning from the illustrations, saying that the lines "look like the trees are moving" and "It must be a windy day!" With their new understandings of how details in art can bring settings to life and even communicate mood, they created their own collaborative work of art to share with others. The power of ArtMaking allows children to think deeply about books, use loose parts to tinker with making art, and communicate their own meaning using art. ArtMaking helps children read illustrations in books, infer meaning, and then use that knowledge to communicate their own message through art. We are excited to step inside the inspiring pages of illustrated children's books with you and discover the possibilities for creating deep levels of understanding as your children learn to observe, infer, and make their own art to derive meaning in their own worlds.

As children's books are always our first source of inspiration, we share Emily Arrow's message from her book *Studio: A Place for Art to Start*. She describes a studio as a place for making art and building dreams. As the subtitle declares, it's "a place for art to start." We invite you to use the pages of this book as inspiration to make a place for art to start in your learning environment—your classroom, studio, home, museum, or library settings. Please bring your children with you on our journey, as they are the readers, makers, artists—the ArtMakers.

WHY ARTMAKING?

Many teachers feel pressure to get their children ready for the next grade level, with reading at the top of the list. Some feel they don't have time and space in their daily instruction to incorporate art, or they think art belongs only in the art teacher's classroom or prekindergarten centers. This might be the result of thinking that the only purpose and value of art in education is encouraging creativity. However, the true importance lies in the fact that making art "reinforces new ways to think" (Goldberg 2014, 36).

ArtMaking is the perfect language to give all children a voice, regardless of age or ability. In ArtMaking, children are invited to "read their worlds" as they learn about images, explore materials and elements of art (colors, lines, shapes, textures, spaces, designs), and communicate their thinking through their own art processes and products. We offer an inquiry cycle (a thinking process that leads to new knowledge through observing, tinkering, connecting, and sharing) that uses artworks by old masters and contemporary artists as well as illustrations from children's picture books as its provocations. As X. Christine Wang and colleagues explain in *Young Children*, "Researchers have advocated for guided approaches that balance free exploration for self-expression with structured development of artistic knowledge and skills" (2019). Thus we seek a balance between open-ended process art and a discipline-based approach that allows children to tinker and apply their knowledge of artists to communicate thinking.

Following the ArtMaking approach, children start with what they see in illustrated books, explore art materials, and study the work of other artists in order to then create their own art. Children make meaning with their visual literacy skills (viewing, understanding, and creating images), and they use the receptive (reading images) and expressive (making images) languages of literacy and art to make connections to illustrations in picture books. Children read the illustrations, infer their meanings, play and tinker with materials, meet artists and make connections to their art, and bring everything together to communicate their own message. The resulting art is a visual representation of their thinking, a synthesis of their understanding created in something new. These skills build a strong literacy foundation for subsequent successful reading and writing. When children engage in ArtMaking, they apply the highest level of the comprehension and visual literacy continua to new art experiences and makerspaces. They are not just making art but making meaning of the book and the world through each phase of the process!

Almost every learning space for young children has art materials and mediums; therefore, you can use what you already have to intentionally grow the communication skills of your children. Each chapter features suggested lessons in which we take you through the four phases of the inquiry cycle of ArtMaking:

- We Are Readers! Observe and Imagine with Picture Books

- We Are Makers! Play and Tinker with Open-Ended Materials

- We Are Artists! Connect and Make with Artists and Artworks

- We Are ArtMakers! Share and Communicate ArtMaking Processes and Products

We Are Readers! Observe and Imagine with Picture Books

In our previous book, *Makerspaces*, we provided a framework for designing provocations in everyday spaces. You select your inspiration and support, choose your main material, select loose parts, and then provide any tools or attachments needed. Here in *ArtMaking*, picture books become the inspiration and support for every lesson, and the art makerspace becomes the tool for children to communicate as they play and tinker with loose parts, explore mediums and artists, and create their own art.

The ArtMaking process begins with phase one of our inquiry cycle: observe and imagine. We start by first choosing a children's book to read aloud, discuss, and retell. Throughout this book, we recommend certain picture books we have found supportive of young children's literacy learning as they begin reading their worlds. If you don't have these titles, you can adapt our lessons to any picture book. As you teach ArtMaking, you'll find even better examples than ours. We can't wait to hear the titles of the picture books you find inspirational!

We Are Makers! Play and Tinker with Open-Ended Materials

We have seen over the years how open-ended materials give children the power to unleash their imaginations and ideas. In *StoryMaking* we observed and documented as children wove imaginative stories while playing and tinkering with materials. Our extensive research continued in *Makerspaces*, showcasing children's learning as they interacted with materials and made projects and artifacts. Simon Nicholson's theory of loose parts aligns to what we have observed between young children and materials: "In any environment, both the degree of inventiveness and creativity, and the possibility of discovery, are directly proportional to the number and kind of variables in it" (1971 5, 6). Our students interact with materials to make stories. They make projects to share their knowledge. They even make art to communicate feelings and thoughts and to share beauty with others. In other words, adults and children both actively seek understanding of our world through interactions with interesting materials. We suggest using loose parts to encourage the following:

- **Scaffold art learning:** Use colorful loose parts to show varying shades, and use textured loose parts to feel contrasts.

- **Inspire:** Use shiny loose parts to demonstrate the reflection of light, and use loose parts to align with a read aloud.

- **Demonstrate subtleties of elements:** Use round loose parts to demonstrate a variety of shapes, and use loose parts in shades of blue to demonstrate intensities in colors.

- **Support:** Trace loose parts when not quite ready to independently represent desired shapes.

- **Communicate:** Use loose parts such as ribbons to show movement, and demonstrate mood by viewing loose parts in different lighting.

We share photographs of art makerspaces—learning spaces to promote long-term investigations of an art element. Each includes inspiration and support, main materials, mediums, loose parts, and tools. We also share tabletop provocations, which are temporary invitations the educator sets up to invoke wonder about upcoming investigations. In each chapter, we recommend certain open-ended materials. If you don't have the particular loose parts we reference, don't worry. Zillions of loose parts can scaffold our children's thinking during ArtMaking. We hope that our suggestions will inspire you to reconsider the loose parts you already have on hand.

We Are Artists! Connect and Make with Artists and Artworks

Inspired by picture books and artwork, we scaffold our young literacy learners and artists as they make and connect with art elements (colors, lines, shapes, textures, spaces), mediums, techniques, and famous artworks. Why art? Because, as Barry Goldberg reports, "making art is a unique form of wordless thinking" (2014, 27). Picture books and artworks grow children into the different phases of making meaning, as children first learn to interpret (receptive language) and then communicate (expressive language) their understanding of visual text. Picture book illustrations provide more-inclusive entry points to learning for children with communication and reading difficulties; the art becomes a tool for their mouths and minds to speak. Art provides another path toward literacy learning, as children get to "select from a wide choice of language practices, a rich array of materials, and an expanding variety of modes for expressing ideas" (Wohlwend 2008).

In each chapter, our connect-and-make section introduces artists and their artwork, techniques, and mediums. We recommend artists and artworks to which our children have connected. If you don't have access to these recommendations, know that all artworks employ each of the art elements, and you can select any artist with whom you have a connection.

We Are ArtMakers! Share and Communicate ArtMaking Processes and Products

We highlight this last phase of our inquiry cycle, share and communicate, by offering documentation panels, works, and words of our ArtMakers. These processes and products demonstrate children's visual literacy proficiency as they summarize and synthesize their learning. When children engage in ArtMaking, they become more proficient in retelling, inferring an illustrator's intent, and determining importance in books. They visualize by tinkering with materials, make connections with artists, and synthesize their thinking to create their own art.

YOU ARE INVITED!

Isn't it refreshing to know you can welcome back creativity, imagination, and inquisitive materials and experiences into your classroom yet still accomplish your literacy goals for your children? ArtMaking provides that balance in a powerful and engaging way by weaving together rich literature and open-ended art materials for children to make and communicate meaning.

You don't have to be an art teacher to implement ArtMaking. The children bring life to the art. You just have to play with the materials and see where they take you. Enjoy the process, open your eyes to the details in illustrations and art, and then linger to consider mood, messages, and deeper meaning. Just sharing perspectives with one another can help your art grow. There are no wrong answers!

We can't wait to share with you all we've learned along the way about visual literacy, loose parts, art, and artists, all coming together in ArtMaking. Each chapter focuses on a particular art element, and the chapters are arranged in a continuum, moving from simple (color, lines, shapes) to more complex (textures, spaces, designs). You can introduce each element in the order it appears in its chapter, or you can pick and choose elements of interest. Each chapter's learning engagements are also arranged from simple to complex, so you can start where your students are and follow the suggestions for next steps.

Each chapter can take up to a month or two to explore, or you can pick and choose what you have time for. We anticipate that each learning engagement will take approximately a week. Feel free, however, to slow down and give the children opportunities to linger and learn more deeply when their curiosities have been ignited, when their interests in the master artists are evident, when they need more knowledge of the process, or when they want to explore and tinker with new materials and mediums. Let's begin to explore new ways to teach reading using art in our own classrooms and studios, which Emily Arrow describes as a "habitat for makers" (2020). We encourage you to open your minds and hearts to making with art and to share your creations with your world of ArtMakers!

"I am cutting to make dashed lines. I want to shape my lines into an animal just like I saw in the book," Fleur expressed as she tinkered with her materials. Aesthetics "includes our response to the world and how we shape it, in images or in lines or colors, in words or gestures" (Gandini et al. 2015, 183). Gaining proficiency in visual literacy empowers our children to shape their worlds.

Chapter 1

Making Meaning Using Visual Literacy and Comprehension Skills

Colors

Lines

Shapes

Textures

Spaces

Teachers of young children have the privilege of introducing them to countless possibilities as they learn to read: adventuring to new places, meeting new friends, crafting stories, and growing their skills. One of the goals of this book is to help you equip young children with skills for navigating their complex worlds of images. Children learn how to "read" visual images using both visual literacy and comprehension skills. Jennifer Serravallo provides a hierarchy of reading goals, with emergent reading at the top of her list. She explains that very young children rely on pictures to make meaning: "They are solidifying an understanding that reading is about making meaning:

understanding what characters do and say; understanding how one event in the story leads to another; having their own ideas and reactions to the text; learning information and connecting information between parts and pages and to their own lives" (2018, 10). The resulting skills serve children as they get older and encounter complex texts, both visual and traditional: activating background knowledge, making connections, visualizing, finding the big idea, and inferring. But first we start with the processes that are unique to visual literacy.

VISUAL LITERACY

We explicitly introduce young children to visual literacy across three dimensions: affective, compositional, and critical (Callow 2008). In the affective dimension, children explore pictures in picture books, derive pleasure from artwork, label components they like, and develop personal interpretations of illustrations—all important components of emergent reading (Sulzby 1994). When children are asked to describe what they see on the page, it requires them to actively construct meaning (Felten 2008). Aesthetics is an important component of this dimension, as children are invited to discover what they like in pictures, articulate why they like it, and develop their own conceptions of beauty. The affective dimension is evidenced when you see children enjoying pictures, labeling components they like, and adding details to their interpretations, such as "I see lots of dark green. Green is my favorite color."

In the compositional dimension, children use art elements (colors, lines, shapes, textures, spaces, design) to learn about the composition of the image. When you ask, "What do you notice in this image?" you might hear a child say, "I see a thick yellow line and a green triangle." As children become more fluent with their visual literacy skills, they learn how to use the elements of art to infer meaning, using clues from the image to consider what the artist is trying to communicate.

In the critical dimension of visual literacy, children learn to evaluate images. It begins when young children notice what the artist may have left out of a picture or when they suggest how the artist could have more effectively used a particular element, technique, or medium. The critiques are supported by children's new knowledge of the elements of art, techniques, and mediums. An example of a child's critique might be, "Van Gogh should have made more spiral lines in his picture. I saw more stars in the night sky than he shows."

COMPREHENSION

We teach our children to access the affective, compositional, and critical dimensions of visual literacy with comprehension skills. Developing fluency in both comprehension and visual literacy skills builds a solid foundation for navigating images and traditional texts.

Research identifies six core comprehension skills every successful reader needs. Stephanie Harvey and Anne Goudvis (2008) remind us that children need a repertoire of experiences over time that allow them to revisit books and construct deeper levels of meaning. Therefore, we don't teach one comprehension skill at a time but rather weave all the comprehension strategies throughout each phase of our ArtMaking process. Here's the order in which we typically reference the comprehension skills during the ArtMaking process:

- **Activate Background Knowledge:** During the first read of our picture books, we intentionally activate background knowledge, which is what a child already knows or brings to the reading event. Some researchers refer to background knowledge as the "foundation of our thinking" (Harvey and Goudvis 2008, 7).

- **Ask and Answer Questions:** Next we introduce new information (how to read an illustration, what the art elements might mean). Young children ask questions to learn about their world, so we celebrate when children ask questions and seek answers.

- **Make Connections:** Children make text-to-self connections during a book's first read, finding commonalities between themselves, the stories, and the illustrations. Later they make text-to-text connections when they meet artists.

- **Retell:** Children build their retelling skills as they practice remembering and recalling details. We review and revisit illustrations and model how to look more deeply and recall details. Students' comprehension increases when they observe carefully and notice and recall details.

- **Infer:** Inferring is referred to as the "bedrock of understanding," so we practice making inferences in each ArtMaking learning engagement (Harvey and Goudvis 2008, 8). Children combine their background knowledge with clues from the image (color, lines, shapes, textures, spaces, design) to infer meaning in the illustrations and artworks.

- **Visualize:** When readers visualize, they construct meaning by creating mental images, using all their senses. Playing and tinkering with concrete representations such as loose parts helps students increase the abstract skill of visualization.

- **Determine Importance:** We purposefully teach children how to identify the main idea in books, illustrations, and artworks. We show them how artists create the main idea using art elements and other techniques, and we have them practice making their own art and sharing their big ideas, building their skill in determining importance.

- **Summarize:** After each learning engagement, children summarize their learning, sharing in their own words the most important things they learned.

- **Synthesize:** When children make art, they synthesize their understandings by combining what they already know and what they've learned in order to create something new. Each of their artworks is a unique and direct reflection of their thinking as well as the synthesis of their learning (Miller 2012, 171). We end each chapter with a synthesis of learning about each art element.

GETTING READY FOR ARTMAKING

We start our process with a picture book to engage children's interest in an image. Picture books can be wordless or can contain text. Either way the images carry the bulk of the meaning, and the book's message can be understood by applying visual literacy skills to the illustrations. Picture books serve many purposes, most of which relate to visual literacy, or "thinking about what images and objects mean, how they are put together, how we respond to or interpret them, [and] how they might function as modes of thought" (Raney 1998, 38).

The first read of the picture book introduces the children to the story and activates their aesthetic sensitivities. We show the beautiful images and discuss what makes the illustrations enjoyable. Our teachers are most successful when they activate the students' background knowledge as they get to know the picture book before focusing on visual literacy skills.

As children become familiar with the picture book and make text-to-self connections, we then select one image to launch ArtMaking. The children study the image, notice and label what they see, retell, ask questions, and more.

Ways ArtMaking Activates Meaning Making

	Comprehension Skill Focus	Visual Literacy Skill Focus
We Are Readers! Observe and Imagine with Picture Books (1 day)	• Retell by zooming in on one picture to observe and label details. • Ask and answer questions.	• Observe/view images. • Derive pleasure. • Discern likes/dislikes. • Develop conception of beauty. • Label/list what you see. • Add details. • Develop personal interpretations. • Analyze meaning (art elements). • Evaluate images. • Create image. • Use image to communicate meaning.
We Are Makers! Play and Tinker with Open-Ended Materials (2–3 days)	• Ask and answer questions. • Infer meaning during 2nd or 3rd reading of the picture. • Visualize how the illustrator/artist represents meaning and consider how you want to represent meaning with loose parts.	
We Are Artists! Connect and Make with Artists and Artworks (1–3 days)	• Make text-to-text connections (illustrations and artists' works). • Ask and answer questions. • Determine the importance (big idea) of illustrations and art.	
We Are ArtMakers! Share and Communicate Thinking (1–2 days)	• Ask and answer questions. • Summarize/synthesize learning when sharing process/product.	

WE ARE READERS! OBSERVE AND IMAGINE WITH PICTURE BOOKS

The first part of the ArtMaking process showcases observation and imagination to increase young children's visual literacy proficiency, or their ability to construct meaning by reading and understanding images. This is demonstrated when children notice details about an image and imagine how their own art could express their understanding of the book or their interests. As children engage in visual literacy learning, they activate their background knowledge to make connections (text-to-self) to the images.

The steps below outline the process to help you plan your focus lessons for each phase. For each ArtMaking session, we gathered the children for a lesson emphasizing a reading skill or an art technique to support their construction of meaning. After the lesson, we invited the children to apply their new knowledge in the art makerspace. Always read the book for enjoyment first. This activates students' learning with curiosity and makes a connection to the aesthetics before you use the book as an anchor text for meaning making.

1. Zoom in on one illustration and list everything you see. Students decode the illustration and **retell** what they see and remember. As Trevor Bryan explains, "Listing everything in a picture is how a visual text is decoded. It is the equivalent to reading every word on a page" (2019, 31). This process begins teaching children the importance of using text evidence to determine meaning. Instead of inserting your interpretations, let the children guide the conversation.

2. Zoom back into the illustration and discuss what you see in the picture to **infer** meaning. Return to the list of everything you see and consider what these details may mean, including what students think about the characters, setting, events, mood, lessons, and big ideas.

3. Introduce an artist and make **text-to-text connections** about the message or visual text details. **Determine the importance** the artist used to inspire making.

4. Encourage children to use the language of art to **summarize and synthesize** their message through their own art. This can include collaborative pieces, a display, photo and video documentation showing students' creative process, or a written or dictated message.

Children find beauty, discover likes and dislikes, and make personal connections when they "read" the illustrations in picture books (affective dimension). They begin to recognize and identify illustrators' uses of art elements, and then to infer meaning (compositional dimension) and figure out how they might make their own pictures even better than the illustrations (critical dimension). They are readers!

WE ARE MAKERS! PLAY AND TINKER WITH OPEN-ENDED MATERIALS

The second part of our inquiry cycle is playing and tinkering. We set up art makerspaces, which are learning spaces to promote long-term investigations of an art element. These spaces include inspiration and support, main materials, mediums, loose parts, and tools. Art makerspaces ensure children have a beautiful space to tinker and make using loose parts and art mediums. In *Makerspaces*, we defined a makerspace as "any place where children of all ages use materials and tools to imagine, play, make, and share their ideas, projects, stories, or thinking" (Thompson and Compton 2020, 1). After being inspired by an illustration, children come to the art makerspace to similarly communicate their thoughts and ideas through art. They use loose parts and open-ended materials to play and tinker with mediums, illustrations, ideas, and materials, figuring out their forms and functions and thinking with their hands to construct their own meaning.

We consistently include the following components in each art makerspace to enhance the invitation to learn and grow as readers, makers, artists, and ArtMakers.

Designing an Art Makerspace	
Inspiration and Support	Children's book illustration, artwork, questions to support children to think deeply about art element
Main Material	Paper, such as construction, copy, card stock, watercolor
Mediums	Crayons, pencils, charcoal, markers, pens, paints, watercolors, ink, pastels
Loose Parts	Open-ended materials that allow children to tinker with art element before committing to the marks on the paper, such as nature objects, wood, paper, plastic, metal, textile, glass
Tools	Paintbrushes and other accessories, such as cups or palettes for mixing paint, easels, hand lens, mirrors, craft sticks for mixing and moving paint

The addition of loose parts offers access points for children who may otherwise have difficulty with the abstract concepts of literacy and art. It's one of the most important components of our art makerspaces. Loose parts scaffold children toward proficiency as they play with their ideas inspired by the illustrations and loose parts (affective dimension); visualize how to represent their ideas (compositional dimension); and decide what parts of the illustrations they think are good and what parts need to be changed (critical dimension). They are makers!

WE ARE ARTISTS! CONNECT AND MAKE WITH ARTISTS AND ARTWORKS

The next phase of our inquiry cycle is connect and make. We introduce artists, both old masters and contemporary, whose art inspires children to make connections between picture book illustrations and artworks (text-to-text), determine the big ideas represented in illustrations and artworks, use their inferring skills to interpret meanings represented in art, and then make artwork of their own. Young children "write their worlds" by figuring out how they can use signs and symbols (colors, lines, shapes, textures, spaces, design) to communicate meaning in art, through both the art processes and their art products.

The following questions may guide your discussions when talking to young children about their art. Since our book is meant to bring children's thinking to the fore, we asked them to represent their art with words in our examples. But in general children do not need to make up a story that aligns with the picture, identify objects, or explain their art. Their art process or product is the message and can stand on its own without words. Rather, the most productive conversations broaden their visual literacy proficiency by talking about what you can actually *see* (colors, lines, shapes, spaces, textures, and design) and giving them language to communicate their thinking about their art (Goldberg 2014). Try not to ask questions or offer compliments that name objects in artworks, such as "Is that your house?" or "I like that flower," which may or may not be the intention of the young artist. When you name an object, children begin to think their art has to be recognizable and has to include "real" things to communicate meaning.

Some examples of supporting children as they develop their retelling skills include:

- "I see [colors, lines, shapes, spaces, textures] [describe actions]." When you state what you see in their art, it honors their thinking and gives them space to have other ideas and to continue experimenting and creating more iterations of their thinking. Examples:

  — "I see the colors running together and making new colors."

  — "I see that Albers placed his squares on top of one another and arranged them from small to big."

- "I notice you [made your marks] by [describe how the marks were made]." This gives children vocabulary for their actions and makes the results of their actions explicit so that they can repeat the techniques discovered along the way. Examples:

  — "I notice how you pressed hard on your crayon to make the purple color darker."

  — "I notice that Seurat put lots of small dots together, called pointillism, to make his pictures."

- "Can you describe how you [drew, sketched, painted, outlined] your [color, lines, shapes, spaces, textures]?" Example:

  — "Can you describe how you drew your horizontal lines?"

- "Let's look at your [or artist's] [artwork, painting, drawing, sketch] together. I see [describe what you see]." Examples:

  — "Let's look at your painting together. I see three colors right next to each other and a thick line across all three colors."

  — "As I look at van Gogh's painting, I see spiral lines in the sky."

- "I notice your [colors, lines, shapes, spaces, textures] are [similar, different, bigger, smaller, closer, brighter] from [artist's]." Examples:

  — "I notice that you spaced your shapes on top of each other just like Klee did in his art."

  — "I see you used warm colors like Monet, but you made your colors more vibrant."

Children make connections to the styles, mediums, and techniques of well-known artists and infer meaning from the art. They find pleasure in recognizing and creating beauty (affective dimension); connect to artists' uses of the elements of art, mediums, techniques, and meanings (compositional dimension); and learn how to evaluate their own and others' art (critical dimension). They are artists!

WE ARE ARTMAKERS! SHARE AND COMMUNICATE ARTMAKING PROCESSES AND PRODUCTS

In ArtMaking, we celebrate process art with its focus on exploring materials and following the students' interests and curiosities (affective dimension) while also integrating learning standards, art elements, and art evaluation (compositional and critical dimensions). We reflect together on what we have learned as a group and how the children have grown as ArtMakers, supporting their development in summarizing and synthesizing. We can celebrate and discuss the process ("What are you discovering as you play and tinker with liquid watercolors?") *and* the product ("How did you use color to communicate your thinking?"), while keeping play at the center of it all. Below are some questions that might guide you as your ArtMakers share and communicate their thinking:

- "What did you learn as you made your art?"

- "How would you like to share your art?"

- "What do you want your audience to see [or imagine] when they look at your [colors, lines, shapes, and so forth]?"

- "What do you want your audience to feel, understand, or learn?"

- "What do you want to teach others when they look at your art?"

- "What message do you want us to know about your art?"

- "What mood are you trying to communicate?"

As our ArtMakers are learning to identify as and think like readers, makers, and artists, a primary goal of ArtMaking is to increase their visual literacy and comprehension skills through picture books and artwork. As children learn about art and literacy, they develop visual literacy proficiency and comprehension skills, and they learn to observe, find pleasure, describe, analyze, interpret, evaluate, and create images as well as increase their aesthetic sensibilities as they develop an appreciation for beauty. They are ArtMakers!

"Look at all the colors! It looks like the rainbows in the CD," a child shared as he joyfully compared the materials. Simple materials and beautiful inspirations can lead to important discoveries, learning, and meaning making while creating in children an appreciation for beauty in their worlds.

Chapter 2

Making Meaning with Color

We begin our exploration of art with the element of color because, as Ann Pelo reminds us, "color anchors us to our world" (2017, 59). Color is connected to every aspect of our lives and is easily accessed and represented everywhere in children's worlds. Color evokes moods, communicates emotions, connects to children's memories, sparks wonders, and invites questions and explorations. Babies and toddlers notice and point to colors even before they can identify the names. Young children engage in visual literacy learning as they activate their background knowledge and make connections to colors they see in illustrations and artwork, as they question how colors are made, as they infer meanings represented by colors, and as they visualize how they want to use color to make their own pictures and drawings. As color is a sensation we perceive when light hits an object and is transmitted to the photoreceptors of the eye (Ceppi and Zini 1998), we coincide our study of color with playful manipulations of light to enlarge and enhance colors, evoke marvel and wonder, and create shadows, movement, and emotion. Adding light and projections magnifies curiosity and wonder "by amplifying phenomena and making them more spectacular" (Reggio Children).

Our first inquiry, as with each element of art, serves as an informal preassessment. We pay attention to exclamations of joy, signs of frustration, and areas for further exploration based on the children's words, actions, and reactions. Once the children have immersed themselves in playing with color and we've gathered information about their curiosities and background knowledge, we can then begin our formal investigation, moving from simple to more complex explorations of color. Whether you spend a month or two on color at the beginning of the year or spread out the investigations across the year, this continuum, represented in a series of documentation stories throughout this chapter, is meant to inspire you as you plan your own color invitations.

Depending on children's existing knowledge and interests, we typically start with an exploration of black and white, as we use these colors as a base to better understand all the other colors (Pelo 2017). Next the children are invited to mix primary colors, stirring and dripping and dabbling as they blend blues, yellows, and reds, recognizing and naming the secondary hues (oranges, greens, purples) they create. Moving along the continuum, we introduce the children to analogous colors, or colors that are close to one another on the color wheel. We invite them to explore warm tones (reds, oranges, and yellows) and cool tones (blues, greens, and purples), choosing their favorites and noticing how the tones make them feel (emotions, mood). Growing their expertise, we move to complementary colors, or colors opposite one another on the color wheel. These colors create bold contrasts and evoke different feelings than the analogous colors. We add complexity by inviting the children to make and name lighter tints (adding white) and darker shades (adding

A Continuum of Color							
Setting the Stage	Black and White	Primary Colors	Warm Tones	Cool Tones	Complementary Colors	Tints and Shades	Color Studies

Setting the Stage

Black and White

Primary Colors

Warm Tones

Cool Tones

Complementary Colors

Tints and Shades

black) of familiar colors, starting with black and white and mixing many shades of gray. Depending on the children's interests, we select particular colors to investigate more deeply. Our final inquiry serves as a summary of our color studies, using children's invented colors (mixed, tinted, shaded, and named) to express movement. The intersection between cognition and imagination is realized with their use of color as they create beauty, express emotion, highlight movement, and represent their perspectives of their worlds (Vecchi 2010a).

MAKING MEANING WITH AN INFORMAL PREASSESSMENT

We began with an invitation for children to explore a spectrum of colors. Through this we assessed what colors they already know, what knowledge of making colors they have, and what specific or favorite colors interest them most. This observational information let us plan the next steps and personalize our color study for each group of children. We selected rainbows first because the entire color spectrum is represented, so we can figure out what children already know about each rainbow color.

Getting Ready for ArtMaking

During the first read of *How the Crayons Saved the Rainbow* by Monica Sweeney, the children discussed what happened and their favorite parts. They made text-to-self connections such as their favorite colors or times they saw a rainbow. "I love rainbows!" "Purple is my favorite color." "I like blue." "I saw a rainbow one day. It was raining." To immerse the children in the aesthetics of color, we went on a rainbow hunt and searched the learning environment for colorful loose parts to sort by color.

Here's an outline of our ArtMaking process introducing children to observing, tinkering, making, and communicating with color. While this chart is provided just once at the beginning of each chapter, it serves as an example of how each investigation can be planned using the ArtMaking process. This initial investigation of color took place over a week.

ArtMaking Process	Lesson Details	Art Makerspace Invitation	Making Meaning Examples
Phase 1 **We Are Readers!** Observe and Imagine	• Return to *How the Crayons Saved the Rainbow* by Monica Sweeney and Feronia Parker Thomas and zoom in on one illustration. • Engage the children in **retelling** the visual image you selected by decoding/listing everything they see.	Invite children to fully explore art makerspace with book inspiration, rainbow loose parts, and crayons and markers.	Retelling: • "I see red and orange." • "That color is yellow." • "I see purple." • "I see green and blue."
Phase 2 **We Are Makers!** Play and Tinker	• Return to illustration and remind them of what they noticed. • Engage children in **inferring** from illustration by using text evidence to support their ideas. • Model using loose parts to help them **visualize** what to make.	Invite children to make with loose parts and the crayons and markers, with a purpose of learning to use the materials.	Inferring: • "We need to work together because the colors are together to make something beautiful." • "We need to get along." • "Rainbows make us happy."
Phase 3 **We Are Artists!** Connect and Make	• Introduce Norman Adams's *Rainbow Painting (1)* and make **text-to-text connections** between the illustration and his painting. • **Determine the importance** of the artist's choices (elements).	Invite children to use their loose parts and crayons/ markers or watercolors with the new purpose of making a mood.	Text-to-text-connections: • "They both have rainbows." • "They both used all the colors." • "They both are beautiful." Inferring mood: • "It makes me feel happy." • "I feel peaceful and calm."

ArtMaking Process	Lesson Details	Art Makerspace Invitation	Making Meaning Examples
Phase 4 **We Are ArtMakers!** Share and Communicate	• Revisit Adams painting and highlight children's artwork. • *Summarize* what was learned about the big idea and mood. Ask, "What do you want others to learn or feel when they look at your picture?"	Invite children to **synthesize** their understanding and make with their loose parts and crayons/markers or watercolors with the new purpose of communicating a big idea or mood.	Summarizing: • "We learned that all the colors are in a rainbow." • "Norman made a rainbow just like our book." • "We can use crayons to make rainbows or whatever is in our imaginations." Synthesizing: • "I made a rainbow. I want my friends to feel happy." (mood)

We Are Readers! Observe and Imagine with *How the Crayons Saved the Rainbow*

How the Crayons Saved the Rainbow introduced the children to many colors of the rainbow. Children were learning to observe illustrations carefully during the first read of the book. The next day, we selected a particular illustration by Feronia Parker Thomas to focus on, to build children's visual literacy acuity. We were drawn to this illustration because it emphasizes using crayons the children were already familiar with. We asked them to study the illustration, retell the events on the page, and label the colors they noticed. "I see red and orange." "That color is yellow." Their comments showed that they were developing their aesthetic sensitivities by responding to illustrations with what they like in art (Walsh 2003).

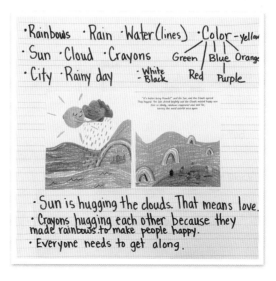

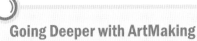

Going Deeper with ArtMaking

Use this QR code or type www.redleafpress.org/amk/2-1.pdf into your browser to Go Deeper.

We Are Makers! Play and Tinker with Open-Ended Materials Sorted by Color

The following day, we started to think about how the illustrator wanted the children to feel by using the reading strategy of inferring. We scaffolded their thinking, leading them toward making meaning by reading the pictures. One child used evidence from the picture to infer that "the sun and cloud should work together because they make beautiful things."

Since this was our first study together and we wanted to assess their knowledge, I asked children to hunt for objects throughout the classroom that represented a color, encouraging them to select colors from the illustrations with which they had made text-to-self connections.

"I found purple. I want to play with it. Then I'll put it on the rainbow." The children gathered, sorted, and tinkered with loose parts they added to their art makerspace.

"I am making my own rainbow." Children tinkered with colored Magna-Tiles on the light box to visualize using colors in their art.

The children explored the materials, both loose parts and the art mediums of crayons and markers, to see what they could imagine making with rainbow colors. Tinkering prior to making art teaches children to visualize and create concrete representations first with materials. Using many materials generates new ways of learning, as demonstrated in the children's organizing, categorizing, and tinkering with the materials of every color in the rainbow (Penfold 2019).

We Are Artists! Connect and Make with Norman Adams

When we gathered for our ArtMaking mini lesson, we viewed a painting to make connections to how artists use color in their work. Since the children all loved images of rainbows, we selected *Rainbow Painting (1)* by Norman Adams from the Tate Britain Museum. Children made text-to-text connections between the colors they saw in the picture book illustrations, the artwork by Adams, and loose parts. To lead the children into higher-order thinking strategies, we asked them to determine the important colors that created a feeling or strong mood, especially bright colors.

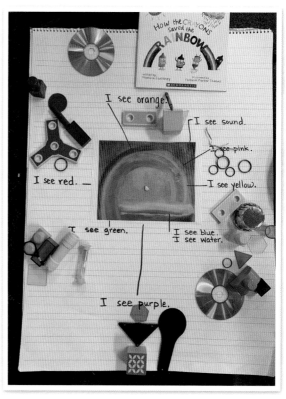

The children then began making in the art makerspace, which now featured images of Adams's work for inspiration. They approached their materials with the purpose of expressing their own moods, just like they learned from the artwork they studied.

Going Deeper with ArtMaking

Use this QR code or type www.redleafpress.org /amk/2-2.pdf into your browser to Go Deeper.

We Are ArtMakers! Share and Communicate with Crayons and Watercolors

After the children made their art, many were ready to share. We summarized our learning about colors, including all the ways children could use color to communicate their emotions, ideas, and stories. Then we invited each child to communicate a summary of what they made and how they wanted us to feel by viewing their art. The children had grown in their literacy, from first viewing an illustration and building on their receptive knowledge to the highest form of comprehension thinking . . . synthesis! They were now using their expressive literacy skills to share what they had created with color.

As a result of our rainbow preassessment, we learned about our children's interests, knowledge of color, visual literacy skills, and aesthetics sensitivities. We were now ready to launch our color study.

Children learned they could use color to communicate with their art. "I made a rainbow. I want my friends to feel happy." —Madelyn, age four

Children learned they could use color to reflect their lives and express emotion. "My rainbow world. A place where I feel happy." —Reed, age four

Going Deeper with ArtMaking

Use this QR code or type www.redleafpress.org/amk/2-3.pdf into your browser to Go Deeper.

MAKING MEANING WITH BLACK AND WHITE COLORS

To launch the investigation of color, we started by exploring black and white. Pelo agrees: "Before launching into the full spectrum of color, stand at its edge with white and black, the beginning and end of color" (2017, 36). This group of three-, four-, five-, and six-year-old children began exploring concepts of light and color with black and white mediums.

Going Deeper with ArtMaking

Use this QR code or type www.redleafpress.org/amk/2-4.pdf into your browser to Go Deeper.

Inspiration for Making Meaning	Materials for Making Meaning
• Book: *Flashlight* by Lizi Boyd or *Color Dance* by Ann Jonas • Art: Black-and-white paintings from Pablo Picasso or Irene Rice Pereira	• Loose parts: Black and white ribbons in a variety of widths or shoelaces • Main material: Black and white construction paper • Medium: Black and white pens in a variety of widths or paint • Tools: Thick and thin paintbrushes, paint cups (if using paint)

We Are Readers! Observe and Imagine with *Flashlight*

As this group of kindergarten children enjoyed the first read aloud of the book *Flashlight* by Lizi Boyd, they were excited to share what colors they noticed in the white light of the flashlight. We selected these illustrations because of the dramatic, contrasting color palette of black and white with hints of color visible only in the light beams. The children retold the details of what they saw and moved quickly to inferring about the mood and how the colors in the book made them feel.

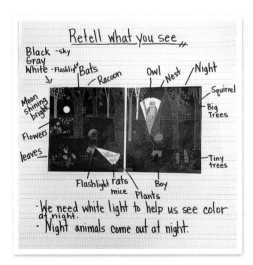

We Are Makers! Play and Tinker with Loose Parts

We cut black and white ribbons of varying widths into pieces so children could visualize what the strokes of paint would look like on their black and white paper. The different widths allowed them to see if they preferred thick or thin strokes and discover how the different paintbrushes could help them achieve what they were imagining. Developing preferences with paint strokes and brushes is another step toward growing the aesthetics dimension of visual literacy.

We Are Artists! Connect and Make with Pablo Picasso

The children were introduced to Pablo Picasso and watched videos of him painting with black and white paint. They viewed his paintings and discussed text-to-text connections between our children's book (*Flashlight*) and the new artworks. This inspired them to return to the makerspace with new ideas for art.

We Are ArtMakers! Share and Communicate with Paint

The children summarized their learning by sharing that they could swirl the color across their page to show movement. One child synthesized that they could use elements of color to represent details in their character's appearance.

"This is my dog. The wind is blowing him away."
—Cai, age four

"This is the body of a dalmatian. This black paper is the thing, but it got switched around. This dalmatian has a black body." —Leigh, age six

Going Deeper with ArtMaking

Use this QR code or type www.redleafpress.org/amk/2-5.pdf into your browser to Go Deeper.

MAKING MEANING WITH PRIMARY COLORS

After exploring the contrasts between black and white, children were excited to experiment with more colors. We started by introducing the primary colors by squishing, mashing, twisting, and mixing two primary colors inside plastic bags. We set up a tabletop provocation to invite children to observe the colors and sort them using images they would encounter in the upcoming read aloud. They asked where the green, orange, and purple picture cards would go, setting the stage perfectly to move forward with primary colors.

Inspiration for Making Meaning	Materials for Making Meaning
• Book: *Bear Sees Colors* by Karma Wilson, illustrated by Jane Chapman, or *A Ball for Daisy* by Chris Raschka • Art: Georges Seurat paintings	• Loose parts: Plastic bingo chips, color paddles, light • Main material: White copy paper • Medium: Tempera paint in yellow, red, and blue • Tools: Round sponge brushes in different sizes, cotton swabs, paint trays

We Are Readers! Observe and Imagine with *Bear Sees Colors*

We chose Jane Chapman's illustrations in the book *Bear Sees Colors* because they led the children on a color-finding journey like our color investigations. The bright colors on the last page gave children the opportunity to truly observe, find, and express their knowledge of colors.

After enjoying the book several times, a child commented, "The bear was finding colors. Red, blue, yellow. . . ."

This beginning discussion led us into enacting our inference skills by exploring the meaning behind the illustrations. We decided that Chapman's message could be "to find beautiful places that make us happy."

We Are Makers! Play and Tinker with Bingo Chips

The children wondered how the green images from the tabletop provocation had been made when there was no green paint. We then modeled mixing the primary colors, previewing the next day's focus lesson of tinkering with mediums and loose parts. A magical buzz of amazement filled the room as they wanted to play and tinker with the paint.

As the children tinkered with the art medium, they were still most interested in mixing the paint to make green. Our focus lesson objective became tinkering with loose parts to discover colors before choosing and mixing paint. They layered translucent bingo chips to reveal new colors. Color paddles and slides with flashlights also provide a great tinkering loose part for mixing colors.

ArtMaking Tip

Only provide two colors at a time so children can learn how to mix to make colors, as Ann Pelo explains: "Using just one or two colors allows the most satisfying exploration of color: it highlights nuances of shading as well as the transformation of colors" (2017, 47). If you provide all primary paint colors at once, the children will want to mix them all, which makes brown.

We Are Artists! Connect and Make with Georges Seurat

We introduced the children to Georges Seurat's impressionist paintings with the video series *Art with Mati and Dada*. They were excited to discover how Seurat's pointillism technique layers blue and yellow dots together to make green. They made text-to-text connections to beautiful places, just like the ones Bear was finding.

We Are ArtMakers! Share and Communicate with Paint

At the end of this investigation, children learned to represent places in their art using color.

"I made a muddy puddle. It is a place of fun!"
—Reed, age three

"I made a zoo." —Shane, age three

MAKING MEANING WITH WARM TONES

As we stepped deeper into the world of colors, we explored analogous colors on one side of the color wheel. A different tabletop provocation signaled to the children that a new investigation was about to take place. They observed the warm tones and images and wondered what colors they could make as they moved the loose parts around.

Inspiration for Making Meaning	Materials for Making Meaning
• Book: *A Day So Gray* by Marie Lamba, illustrated by Alea Marley, or *Hike* by Pete Oswald • Art: Claude Monet sunset paintings, such as *San Giorgio Maggiore at Dusk*	• Loose parts: Warm tones of Magna-Tiles or colored index dividers cut into shapes or strips • Main material: White canvas, white butcher paper • Medium: Oil pastels

We Are Readers! Observe and Imagine with *A Day So Gray*

While enjoying the first reading of *A Day So Gray* by Marie Lamba, we discussed text-to-self connections, such as "a time I went sledding in the snow." Alea Marley's illustrations provided the perfect layers of warm tones, and children expressed their knowledge of mixing colors such as yellow and red. They also began sensing the mood from this side of the color wheel. After the next reading, they retold everything they saw by zooming in on one illustration of a sunset and listing all the colors they noticed.

We Are Makers! Play and Tinker with Magna-Tiles and Light

As we returned to the book, we began to infer the meaning of the illustration. The children used text evidence and shared their thinking about why the mood was warm, comfy, or cold. They tinkered with Magna-Tiles to imagine how they could layer warm tones before tinkering with the oil pastels.

ArtMaking Tip

If children have never used a specific art medium, provide play and tinker invitations for that medium by itself to build fluency. These early explorations can add aesthetics to other makerspaces.

We Are Artists! Connect and Make with Claude Monet

The children compared the illustration with Claude Monet's sunset paintings. Monet studied light and color in his works, so portraying different times of day highlighted the changes in both color and light. The children made text-to-text connections, noticing how each image used warm colors that created a "comfy" and "cozy" mood. They made their marks with oil pastels, using the warm colors on the color wheel.

We Are ArtMakers! Share and Communicate with Oil Pastels

The children wanted to synthesize their learning by creating a comfy corner that would make them feel warm and safe. We designed a documentation display of their Monet-inspired work. We summarized all that we had learned and wrote a documentation story together to teach others about our process and our art's intent.

Going Deeper with ArtMaking

Use this QR code or type www.redleafpress.org/amk/2-6.pdf into your browser to Go Deeper.

MAKING MEANING WITH COMPLEMENTARY COLORS

The color wheel was complete, and we could now investigate the role of complementary colors in ArtMaking. Sometimes when studying a topic, children become interested in an image, and then a new exploration emerges. This was the case for this group of three- and four-year-olds.

Inspiration for Making Meaning	Materials for Making Meaning
• Book: *Bats* by Elizabeth Carney • Art: Mark Rothko paintings	• Loose parts: Paper strips in varying widths • Main material: White construction paper • Medium: Tempera paint cakes • Tools: Paintbrushes

We Are Readers! Observe and Imagine with *Bats*

After children expressed interest in learning about bats, we lingered on an image of a night sky. They loved the beauty of the colors, making text-to-self connections between the sunset- and sunrise-colored canvases they had created in a previous study. They retold facts and also listed all the details they noticed in the photograph.

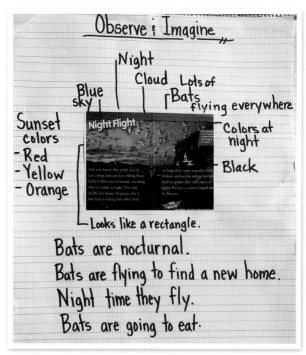

We Are Makers! Play and Tinker with Paper Strips

Children inferred that the photograph was teaching them that bats are helpful because of how many bugs they eat. With this big idea in our minds, we tinkered with paper strips of complementary colors.

We Are Artists! Connect and Make with Mark Rothko

We introduced the children to Mark Rothko, an abstract expressionist painter who used color to express feelings and emotions. His large works evoke emotion and invite the viewer to linger. The children immediately made text-to-text connections between the horizontal bands of color and the night sky. They determined the importance of choosing colors, as they could represent the time of day.

We Are ArtMakers! Share and Communicate with Tempera Paint Cakes

The children summarized that they could layer colors to create a mood. One child synthesized that they created a "gloomy" and "spooky" scene to teach about bats, while another child's purpose was to teach others facts about cats, using a "rainbow sky."

"This is a spooky and gloomy place where bats live in caves and come out to eat at night." —Henry, age five

"Cats meow, meow and they run very fast. They purr and give love." —Madelyn, age four

MAKING MEANING WITH TINTS AND SHADES

Having fully discovered the colors represented across the color wheel, we were ready to explore tints and shades. We returned to the opposite ends of the spectrum (black and white) to uncover the tints and shades the children could make.

Inspiration for Making Meaning	Materials for Making Meaning
• Book: *A Day So Gray* by Marie Lamba, illustrated by Alea Marley • Art: Alma Thomas gray paintings, such as *Gray Night* and *Delias in Fall*	• Loose parts: Bathroom and mosaic tiles • Main material: Canvas • Medium: Tempera paint • Tools: Paintbrushes

We Are Readers! Observe and Imagine with *A Day So Gray*

Returning to beloved books reinforces good reading habits, as children gain fluency with repeated readings. This is why we read *A Day So Gray* again for inspiration in creating shades (adding black into white) or tints (adding white into black) of gray. After reading, the children zoomed in on the Alea Marley illustration with the less-vivid colors of winter. They listed everything they saw and then expressed their likes *and* dislikes of the image, showing their progress in the aesthetics dimension of visual literacy.

We Are Makers! Play and Tinker with Mosaic Tiles

Children tinkered with bathroom and mosaic tiles, inspired by shades of gray from books and paint chips. They placed, stacked, matched, and mixed the colors.

We Are Artists! Connect and Make with Alma Thomas

Next we introduced Alma Thomas, an artist who studied color theory and represented colors found in nature. She once said, "Color is life. Light is the mother of color" (Smithsonian American Art Museum). The children studied how she placed her shades of gray on paper. They made text-to-text connections from Marley's layers of gray colors and snow and what they described as Thomas's "stacks of colors."

We Are ArtMakers! Share and Communicate with Tempera Paint

The children summarized that they could make light tints and dark shades of gray by mixing in different amounts of white or black paint. One child synthesized her learning by explaining that the shades of gray could represent "a cloudy day."

"I made a sunrise on a cloudy day. I made a lighter tint when I added white. But then I made more black to make it darker, like a sunrise on a cloudy day."
—Madelyn, age four

MAKING MEANING WITH COLOR STUDIES

At this point in the continuum, we began to dig deeper and investigate particular colors the children were most interested in. We invited children to a table-top provocation to make colors using food coloring, water, and eyedroppers. The excitement and wonder of their oohs and aahs was contagious!

Inspiration for Making Meaning	Materials for Making Meaning
• Book: *The Color Monster* by Anna Llenas • Art: Alma Thomas's colorful paintings	• Loose parts: Paint chips • Main material: White watercolor paper • Medium: Food coloring and water or liquid watercolors • Tools: Eyedroppers, ice cube trays, and brushes

We Are Readers! Observe and Imagine with *The Color Monster*

We read the book *The Color Monster* for the first time and practiced retelling by listing everything we saw in one illustration. "We see black, gray, yellow that's happy, blue that's sad, red and green that makes me calm," the children chimed in. For the second reading, we zoomed back into an illustration and began to infer the illustrator's message. Using clues from the picture, we decided that the message was "We can feel happy by using colors."

We Are Makers! Play and Tinker with Paint Chips

We modeled using paint chips to tinker and visualize color before the children placed their strokes of color across the paper. They played and sorted the paint chips by color, shape, and size.

We Are Artists! Connect and Make with Alma Thomas

We returned to the work of Alma Thomas, this time viewing her colorful paintings. Then the children created their own colorful nature-inspired art.

We Are ArtMakers! Share and Communicate with Liquid Watercolors

The ArtMakers learned they could mix and experiment with color to inspire future investigations. Children synthesized their discoveries by sharing what they learned about color, their meanings, and new wonderings.

Going Deeper with ArtMaking

Use this QR code or type www.redleafpress.org /amk/2-7.pdf into your browser to Go Deeper.

"I made a rainbow because I love all the colors."
—August, age three

SYNTHESIZING OUR LEARNING ABOUT COLOR

To celebrate and synthesize our learning about color, we reflected on all the hues we learned to identify, make, and use to express our own emotions, big ideas, and thinking. We turned to artist Helen Frankenthaler to help us celebrate our new understandings. We noticed the vibrant colors that fill her canvas. We studied pictures of her working in her studio and loved how she used sponges and even mops to paint. We tried our own smaller versions of her style of painting, using ribbons to splash color across the page. This is the story of how we created an artwork together, inspired by Frankenthaler and her love of colors.

We read *Dancing through Fields of Color*, Frankenthaler's story, and the children noticed how she poured and moved the paint across the canvas. Each child selected two colors to mix to make their own unique color. They looked through books to find ideas for naming their color.

August made a shade she named "Rumble Tumble Pink." She got the idea from the book *Swatch*, about a girl who captured colors. She studied the art to help her visualize what she was going to paint. We used ribbons to tinker with how poured paint looked on our paper.

With their new colors, the children were ready to paint like Frankenthaler! Each child poured paint out of their cups onto the shared blank canvas. Then each selected a tool, using mops, sponges, and bottle brushes to move the paint around. Soon they noticed the colors merging and blending to make new colors. They made connections to how Frankenthaler painted. More important, they discovered that they made something beautiful as a team of ArtMakers!

This documentation panel celebrates the culmination of our color study. Young ArtMakers observed and labeled colors they identified in illustrations as a first step in their visual literacy learning. They increased the complexity of their learning when they played and tinkered with loose parts and when they visualized using colors to represent emotions, moods, and thinking. They made text-to-text connections between picture book illustrations and master artists' works as they inferred the artists' meanings. We agree with Pelo when she states, "Color holds story, metaphor, and emotion for both children and adults" (2017, 59). Our children used color to show their increased aesthetic sensitivities to make what they liked, communicate their feelings, show movement, state lessons, tell stories, and represent their lives.

"I made a castle for a princess with spiral, straight, squiggly, zigzag, and stacked lines." Some consider aesthetics to be a sensibility that defines how people intentionally show what they value, appreciate, and care about (castles, princesses). It's a playful way of being receptive to elaboration, exaggeration, and emphasis (spiral, straight, squiggly, zigzag, and stacked lines); showing understanding; and communicating (sharing with us exquisite artwork).

Chapter 3

Making Meaning with Lines

We selected lines as the next element of art to study, as young children naturally use lines when they begin making marks, typically scribbling. As children develop fluency in forming lines, they are growing skills for letter formation and building the potential for writing fluency. Art offers an alternative language for communication, and for children who find handwriting and letter formation difficult, our study of lines provides an easy access point toward increasing their visual literacy proficiency while simultaneously developing their fluency with lines and future letter formation.

This continuum, represented in a series of documentation stories throughout the chapter, is meant to guide you as you begin planning your own line invitations.

We first introduce straight lines as children make large marks across their papers, often to represent movement, action, or directionality. While discovering and playing with these lines, children next learn about vertical, horizontal, and diagonal strokes, which are required for letter formation. Differentiating between thick and thin lines enables children to visualize different ways to represent places, times of day, and characters. We next explore styles of lines, specifically dotted and dashed lines. These types of lines require more control and intentionality than simply making straight and weighted lines. We are also adding complexity to interpreting meaning of these lines, as children become more proficient at inferring. Next we introduce organic lines and contour lines, which give children opportunities to develop precision as they follow the outlines of shapes. Finally, the children play with spirals that naturally occur in nature (nautilus shells, sliced head of cabbage) and discover how varying spirals (size, color, thickness) and other curved lines convey weather, wind, mood, stars, movement, and sound. Finally, we show children that they can use all kinds of lines to create patterns. They begin to notice patterns everywhere in their worlds. Since patterns and connections are at the heart of aesthetics (Vecchi 2010a), we also focus on noticing and creating beauty in their worlds, using lines. Our culminating inquiry combines all sorts of lines as children enact their aesthetic sensibilities and make their version of beauty with lines.

MAKING MEANING WITH AN INFORMAL PREASSESSMENT

We began with an initial invitation to assess children's existing ability to comprehend lines and use them to express themselves. We wanted to see what lines they notice, how they describe the lines, and how they use lines in their art. We then began building a list of lines that we noticed. Brainstorming what to call each line created a consistent vocabulary to build deeper meaning with our lines.

A Continuum of Lines							
Setting the Stage	Straight Lines	Horizontal and Vertical Lines	Line Weight (Thick and Thin)	Line Style (Dotted and Dashed)	Organic Lines	Curved and Spiral Lines	Lines to Create Patterns

Setting the Stage

Straight Lines

Horizontal and Vertical Lines

Thick and Thin Lines

Dotted and Dashed Lines

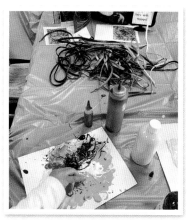

Organic Lines

Curved and Spiral Lines

Lines to Create Patterns

Getting Ready for ArtMaking

During our first reading of *In a Jar* by Deborah Marcero we discussed what happened and our favorite parts. We allowed for text-to-self connections to emerge, such as "I like to go and explore" and "I have been on a boat on the water" and "We collect things in jars too." We also observed which images the children liked most. We invited the children to draw lines so we could observe their prior knowledge.

 Use this QR code or type www.redleafpress.org/amk/3-t.pdf into your browser to view the chart online, or find the chart in the appendix on page 163.

We Are Readers! Observe and Imagine with *In a Jar*

When the children first heard the book *In a Jar*, they were enchanted by how the main character collects things from nature, just like they do in school. We invited children to notice and name their favorite lines from Deborah Marcero's lively illustrations. We were drawn to the illustration of the shoreline because it represents a variety of lines and uses lines to make patterns. The children connected to their previous study of colors by noticing "warm colors." They also began noticing "rainbow lines," "wavy lines," and "lines across the sky." We invited children to make lines to assess their prior knowledge. We provided crayons, colored pencils, and markers to observe the children's comfort and interest in making lines and using the art mediums. We noticed that some made spiral lines while others made marks or scribble-like lines, beginning to play with moving their crayon or pencil across the paper.

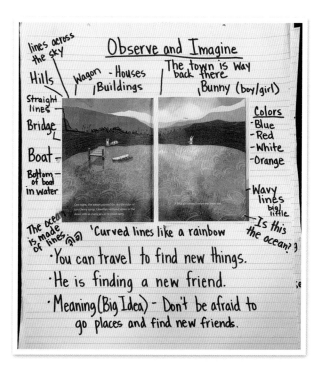

We Are Makers! Play and Tinker with Objects Found in Nature

We wanted children to begin noticing lines not just in one illustration but in the world around us. The children made strong connections to the character from *In a Jar* and his love of exploring the great outdoors, so that's where we went! They noticed lines in branches, as fallen trees, on bark, and even on mushrooms. We gathered small, safe nature loose parts (bark, sticks, leaves) to play and tinker with making lines.

ArtMaking Tip

For children with little knowledge of lines, we scaffold by providing examples of lines and gems to follow the pattern, to expose them to how lines move and are formed.

We Are Artists! Connect and Make with Vincent van Gogh

The children viewed one of the wheat field paintings from Vincent van Gogh and immediately made text-to-text connections to the lines. "There are the squiggly lines here too." Van Gogh is known for his use of lines as well as the outdoor places he chose to paint, most often in nature. "This is a field." Identifying the place helped them understand that they could represent places when they went to make their own art.

We Are ArtMakers! Share and Communicate with Crayons, Colored Pencils, and Markers

We summarized everything we'd learned during this introduction to lines. Some children said, "There are lines in our books." "We can use lines to make places." Then they returned to the art makerspace and shared what they'd made with one another. Michaela and Joshua used lines for making characters, while Reed detailed her setting with lines.

"I made a bird with curved lines and zigzag lines." —Michaela, age four

"I used squiggly lines to make a sunset." —Reed, age three

"I made a picture of the boys racing with spiral and squiggly lines." —Joshua, age four

ArtMaking Tip

There are various ways to represent children's words in their art. Adding words shows them that art communicates meaning, but art does not necessarily need words to communicate thinking. We have found sticky notes helpful, as they can be removed so the art stands on its own.

MAKING MEANING WITH STRAIGHT LINES

Straight lines were first on our continuum because straight lines invite big-motor movements as children make marks and build their confidence in making lines. Large straight lines easily move from one end of the paper to the other. To spark curiosity and excitement for this investigation, we set up a tabletop provocation for children to wonder, play, and tinker with the lines and images they would be formally introduced to later. "Look at my colorful picture I made with light!" "I made my line bend." "Lines are all in my picture!" were just some of the celebrations that emerged as they tinkered with lines and blocks.

Inspiration for Making Meaning	Materials for Making Meaning
• Book: *They All Saw a Cat* by Brendan Wenzel • Art: *Transverse Line* by Wassily Kandinsky	• Loose parts: Pipe cleaners • Main material: White copy paper • Medium: Charcoal sticks and pencils

We Are Readers! Observe and Imagine with *They All Saw a Cat*

During the first read of *They All Saw a Cat*, the children were fascinated by how the cat kept changing its appearance. "Why does the cat look scary now?" and "Why does the cat look like dots?" The children continued to wonder and ask questions as we zoomed in on an illustration, studied the lines, and tried out a new medium.

We zoomed in on the illustration with the many lines and patterns showing the cat in different ways. This image by Brendan Wenzel provided the perfect opportunity to grow our list of lines, retell everything we noticed, and focus attention on straight lines. "This line looks like a firework," one child said as she traced her finger across the lively lines. We agreed that this was the perfect name and added it to our collaborative chart. "This line goes up and down," another child said and quickly went to the page to show text evidence of all the lines he remembered. We agreed to name them "zigzag" lines. We discussed how we all see things differently and how it's important to think about what you would like people to see as you make your art.

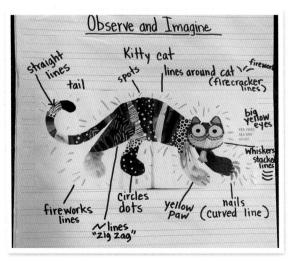

We Are Makers! Play and Tinker with Pipe Cleaners

The children were excited to try out their new art medium, charcoal, using their favorite book pages for inspiration. They were also excited to play with loose parts, including pipe cleaners.

Since the children had never worked with charcoal sticks, we invited them to use pipe cleaners to help visualize what they wanted to make before using the charcoal.

We Are Artists! Connect and Make with Wassily Kandinsky

We then introduced the children to Wassily Kandinsky, who considered lines a basic element in all his works. He believed that the art elements were directly related to meaning in an artwork. The children used their comprehension and visual literacy skills as they studied Kandinsky's lines to find meaning: "That looks like a butterfly" (making connections); "I see eyelashes" (noticing details); "I think that is a sun setting" (inferring). The children considered what they wanted others to see by making straight, angled, and other lines with charcoal.

We Are ArtMakers! Share and Communicate with Charcoal

Once the children finished making their marks across the white paper, they rushed over, ready for us to capture their words that expressed what they wanted everyone to see in the lines in their art.

Fleur and Cai learned they could use lines to represent settings (place, time of day) and objects found in nature.

"I want people to see a night sky." —Fleur, age four

"I want people to see a bird's nest." —Cai, age three

MAKING MEANING WITH HORIZONTAL AND VERTICAL LINES

Next was our study of horizontal and vertical lines, which would provide a strong foundation for letter formation and representation. Vertical and horizontal lines add intentionality and directionality (up/down and left/right) to line formation. A tabletop provocation invites children to play with dominoes to see what lines they notice and what they create.

Inspiration for Making Meaning	Materials for Making Meaning
• Book: *Last Stop on Market Street* by Matt de la Peña, illustrated by Christian Robinson • Art: *Broadway Boogie Woogie* by Piet Mondrian	• Loose parts: Dominoes, strips of construction paper • Main material: White copy paper • Medium: Markers • Tools: Rulers

We Are Readers! Observe and Imagine with *Last Stop on Market Street*

Once the children were familiar with *Last Stop on Market Street*, we selected an illustration by Christian Robinson that had lots of vertical and horizontal lines, showing a bus on a city street. We were drawn to his illustrations because of the vivid and broad lines used to make signs, buildings, and vehicles. The children initially made many text-to-self connections, like "I ride a bus" or "I live in a city too!" But then they got excited as they started noticing the lines. "That's a line for the street." "I see lines on the bus."

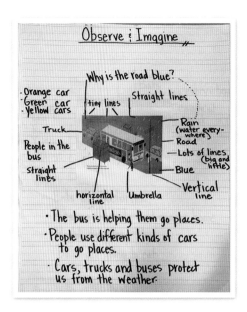

We Are Makers! Play and Tinker with Dominoes and Strips of Paper

The children had fun playing with dominoes and strips of paper. They began to visualize their own streets and scenes they could make. Because some of the children tried to use the strips of paper to draw lines, we also introduced rulers for those who were interested.

We Are Artists! Connect and Make with Piet Mondrian

Piet Mondrian often used lines to represent nature, city streets, and other settings. When he moved to New York to escape World War II, he fell in love with the city and its streets, life, and music. *Broadway Boogie Woogie* was inspired by the New York streets and inspired the children to connect to their own city streets.

"I'm making that," referring to one of Mondrian's works of art. The child had selected it based on his sense of aesthetics and what appealed to his senses.

Making text-to-text connections between the illustrations in *Last Stop on Market Street* and Piet Mondrian's *Broadway Boogie Woogie*: "All the red lines. They are the decorations in my streets."

We Are ArtMakers! Share and Communicate with Markers

After learning that artists can represent cityscapes in their art, the children created their own works and summarized their learnings. For some of our older students, rulers led to all kinds of discoveries of lines (parallel lines, diagonal lines) and more, all while emulating Mondrian's representations of his world.

"It's called Sarasota. It's a park and a circus. The straight lines is just like him [Mondrian]. They are the streets to get to the circus [circles]." —Emmet, age four

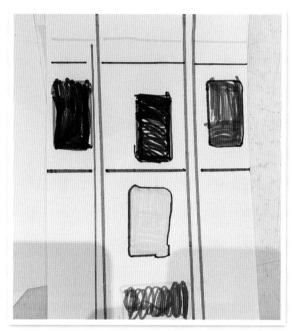

"This is my street. My house is yellow." —Landon, age four

ArtMaking Tip

Another classroom used electrical tape to allow three- and four-year-old children to tinker with horizontal and vertical lines.

MAKING MEANING WITH LINE WEIGHT
(THICK AND THIN)

The children expressed interest in skies, including sunsets and night skies, after studying Monet and wondering how they could represent nature using lines. Therefore, following the children, we took our inspiration from a nonfiction text about beautiful lines that light up the northern skies. The learning space was set to stimulate all the senses in exploring this topic and noticing the thick and thin lines that naturally occur as polar lights.

Inspiration for Making Meaning	Materials for Making Meaning
• Book: *Glow in the Dark: Nature's Light Spectacular* by Katy Flint, illustrated by Cornelia Li • Art: *Allah* by Ismail Gulgee	• Loose parts: Tulle fabric strips • Main material: Black construction paper • Medium: Chalk pastels

We Are Readers! Observe and Imagine with
Glow in the Dark: Nature's Light Spectacular

We read only one page of the nonfiction text to soak in all the facts and study the illustration by Cornelia Li. The illustrator beautifully captured the thin and thick lines that can naturally occur in the polar region. "The lights are so pretty!" "Look at how they glow," the children whispered as they stared at the glowing light image. We projected the page so children could really study the illustration and retell what they heard and saw. "It's shiny." "I see a yellow river." "I see green and purple." "I see an explorer." "There are squiggly lines in the sky!" They were also eager to explore the new chalk pastels.

We Are Makers! Play and Tinker with Tulle

The following day, we reviewed the illustration and inferred that it intended to make us feel "calm" and "relaxed" and to express the idea that "nature was full of magic." We modeled stretching and moving thin and thick pieces of tulle across the page to help the children visualize their lines and tinker with their placement before making lines on the paper.

We Are Artists! Connect and Make with Ismail Gulgee

Next we introduced the children to Ismail Gulgee, as his paintings often show actions, energy, and flow with thick and thin lines. We made text-to-text connections between the lines in the sky in the *Nature's Light Spectacular* illustration and the lines moving across the Gulgee painting. "They both float." "They both are like squiggly lines." The children were figuring out that they could use squiggly lines to show movement, just like the artists.

We Are ArtMakers! Share and Communicate with Chalk Pastels

Joshua and Cai summarized that they learned that lines can show action. Madelyn has learned that she can visually represent her imagination through art.

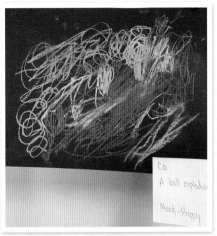

"I made a rocket. The mood is happy and the lines are blasting." —Joshua, age four

"I made a ball exploding!" —Cai, age three

"I made a forest with rainbow grass." —Madelyn, age four

MAKING MEANING WITH LINE STYLE (DOTTED AND DASHED)

We took our inspiration once more from the night skies and followed the children's interest in learning more about stars. We studied dotted and dashed lines and how we could make stars. We set up a tabletop provocation for children to explore constellations and use lines to make images in the night sky. Children began inferring what the lines represented—"This looks like a circle" and "This looks like the Big Dipper"—and wondered how they could draw like this too!

Inspiration for Making Meaning	Materials for Making Meaning
• Book: *What We See in the Stars* by Kelsey Oseid • Art: *Composition* by Bart van der Leck	• Loose parts: Circle metallic gems and silver party bag ties • Main material: Black construction paper • Medium: Chalk markers • Tools: Scissors, playdough, mirrors

We Are Readers! Observe and Imagine with *What We See in the Stars*

We selected a book about constellation patterns. When we focused on a particular illustration by Kelsey Oseid, the children immediately commented, "Those are straight lines in the stars," sharing their previous knowledge from the class line chart. We prompted them to look carefully at the lines and explain how they were different from the ones we learned from Kandinsky. "They have spaces in them." "This one has dots." We honored their powerful observations and labeled them "dotted and dashed lines" on our class line chart.

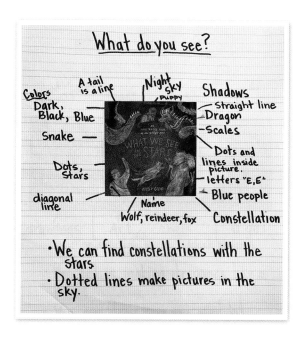

We Are Makers! Play and Tinker with Metallic Gems and Bag Ties

Children used silver playdough on mirrors, playing and tinkering with dotted and dashed lines with the reflected materials. Some children cut metallic bag ties into various lengths and tinkered with metallic gems, using lines to make an image. When they had concrete representations of what they wanted to create, they practiced with chalk markers to make their images come to life.

We Are Artists! Connect and Make with Bart van der Leck

We turned to artist Bart van der Leck's dotted and dashed lines. Van der Leck started his career working with stained glass, and you can see this influence in many of his works. We noticed that most of his lines were dotted and dashed, similar to stained glass windows. The children tried to visualize a whole picture from the dashed lines. "What is that?" "I see a goat!" one child shouted. "Oh yeah, I see it now," another child agreed. They were making text-to-text connections, seeing pictures from their schema (memory) to form a picture in their mind. "It's like when you watch the clouds and see an animal." The children were discovering that there can be multiple meanings and interpretations of art.

We Are ArtMakers! Share and Communicate with Chalk Markers

The children summarized what they learned as they expressed what they wanted people to see when viewing their dotted and dashed lines. All the art was proudly displayed, with their words holding an equal place of value to the art they created. They shared with their friends what they made and what it meant to them.

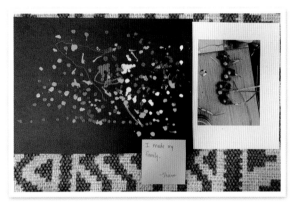

"I made my family." —Shane, age three

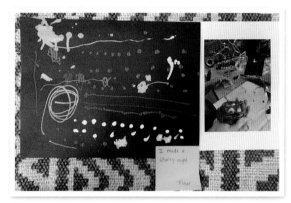

"I made a starry night." —Fleur, age four

MAKING MEANING WITH ORGANIC LINES

Next we were ready to study organic lines. A table-top provocation with projected images of swirling paint covered the walls, inviting children to notice, trace, and interact with the art.

Inspiration for Making Meaning	Materials for Making Meaning
• Book: *When I Draw a Panda* by Amy June Bates • Art: *Autumn Rhythm* or any drip paintings by Jackson Pollock	• Loose parts: Shoelaces • Main material: White butcher paper, white construction paper • Medium: Tempera paint • Tools: Squeeze bottles

We Are Readers! Observe and Imagine with *When I Draw a Panda*

By this time, the children were noticing lines everywhere. During our first read of *When I Draw a Panda*, the children immediately connected to the "swirling" and "twirling" lines in chalk. We added their new vocabulary to our line chart, highlighting lines showing movement.

When we zoomed in on an illustration, we asked, "What do you think is happening in this picture?" They noticed that the lines were moving across the page and inferred that they were dancing.

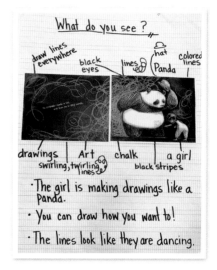

We Are Makers! Play and Tinker with Shoelaces

The children wanted their lines to dance on their paper too. We invited them to visualize what this might look like by tinkering with shoestrings.

We Are Artists! Connect and Make with Jackson Pollock

We introduced the children to Jackson Pollock, a painter who has gained recognition for his poured, dripped, and painted organic lines on large canvases. The children immediately made text-to-text connections by explaining, "He makes his lines move across the paper too!"

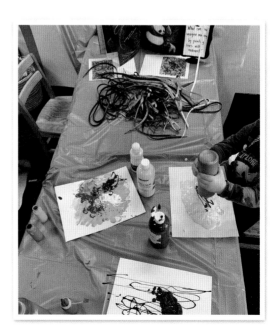

Going Deeper with ArtMaking

Use this QR code or type www.redleafpress.org/amk/3-1.pdf
into your browser to Go Deeper.

We Are ArtMakers! Share and Communicate with Tempera Paint

The children summarized that they could make organic lines by moving their tools around the paper as they painted. Both Henry and Bowman understood that they could use lines to show movement in their paintings.

"I made a jungle with a lot of trees blowing in the wind."
—Henry, age five

"This is an ocean with a lot of waves." —Bowman, age four

ArtMaking Tip

One class used squeeze bottles on a collaborative drip painting to show movement. Squeeze bottles provide an easy way for children to achieve the organic lines seen in Pollack's art, as they can control the flow of paint and move it around the canvas.

Going Deeper with ArtMaking

Use this QR code or type www.redleafpress.org/amk/3-2.pdf
into your browser to Go Deeper.

MAKING MEANING WITH CURVED AND SPIRAL LINES

Next we were ready to investigate curved and spiral lines. Children were beginning to understand how lines create a sense of movement and how they could use those lines to create more details in their settings. To add excitement, we designed a small world makerspace, a place where children invent their own landscapes and inhabitants, where children could play and create stories under an inspiring night sky.

Inspiration for Making Meaning	Materials for Making Meaning
• Book: *Your Name Is a Song* by Jamilah Thompkins-Bigelow, illustrated by Luisa Uribe • Art: *Starry Night* by Vincent van Gogh	• Loose parts: Gel bracelets cut apart, bead necklace pieces • Main material: White watercolor paper • Medium: Watercolor pencils • Tools: Thin brushes

We Are Readers! Observe and Imagine with *Your Name Is a Song*

After reading *Your Name Is a Song*, the children asked why there were lines around the people in the street and in the sky. To help answer and launch our investigation of curved and spiral lines, we zoomed in on one of Luisa Uribe's illustrations. We were drawn to this illustration because it used lines not only to create movement but also to represent sound, such as singing, speaking, or playing music. "Why is there this line [finger movements that went round and round] in that sky?" one child asked. This was a great opportunity to label "spiral lines" and then continue our discussion of the picture.

We Are Makers! Play and Tinker with Gel Bracelets

After lingering with our questions, we demonstrated beating a drum over a plastic-covered bowl with small loose parts. The children quietly observed and noticed the objects moving every time we played the drum. This is a perfect connection to science, proving how we cannot see sound but we can hear and feel it. We discussed how artists can represent sound with lines. When we returned to the illustration, we inferred that the characters were playing music or singing loudly. During the focus lesson, we tinkered with gel bracelets under black lights and strings of beads on the light box, along with the peg people characters from the small world makerspace. A day later, we demonstrated how to use the new medium of watercolor pencils.

We Are Artists! Connect and Make with Vincent van Gogh

We then introduced the children to the famous painting *Starry Night* by Vincent van Gogh. They immediately made text-to-text connections in the ways both artists used lines in the sky to represent stars. They wanted to share their appreciation of the beauty they saw (affective dimension): "I like the swirl sky." "This is something beautiful." They were eager to create pieces showcasing beauty using the new watercolor pencils.

We Are ArtMakers! Share and Communicate with Watercolor Pencils

The children summarized that they could use spiral lines not only to represent beauty, like van Gogh, but also to show movement. Reed synthesized that she could reflect a silly mood by placing curved and "wiggly" lines on a picture of her belly to represent her stomach growling.

"I made circles like van Gogh." —Campbell Grace, age three

"This is me with a hungry tummy." —Reed, age four

MAKING MEANING WITH LINES TO CREATE PATTERNS

Once again the room was transformed, and we invited children to play with light and be inspired by the projected images from our new picture book. We were ready to combine all our knowledge of lines and use them in new ways to create patterns.

Inspiration for Making Meaning	Materials for Making Meaning
• Book: *You're Snug with Me* by Chitra Soundar, illustrated by Poonam Mistry • Art: *The Last Salmon Run* by Alfredo Arreguin	• Loose parts: Patterned washi tape, yarn • Main material: White copy paper • Medium: Gel pens

We Are Readers! Observe and Imagine with *You're Snug with Me*

The prekindergarten and kindergarten-aged children expressed their love of the projected images they had been playing in all morning and began to ask where they came from. After reading *You're Snug with Me*, they zoomed in on an illustration and immediately began shouting, "Wow! Look at all those lines." The illustrations by Poonam Mistry showed repetition, using the same type of lines over and over to create patterns.

We Are Makers! Play and Tinker with Washi Tape

The children were still timid to create intricate lines, so we provided patterned washi tape for them to cut and place into patterns on their paper. Lifting and repositioning the tape helped them visualize the image they wanted to make. We gave yarn to older children who wanted to make patterns with loops.

ArtMaking Tip

Setting up different tabletop provocations for making patterns allows children to tinker with making patterns in a concrete way, which builds their confidence. Here children used figurines, shells, and transparent lines to make patterns on the overhead projector.

We Are Artists! Connect and Make with Alfredo Arreguin

We chose artwork from Alfredo Arreguin because he uses line patterns to create beautiful images just like our picture book. The children discussed how to make settings using dotted and dashed lines. They made text-to-text connections, noticing that the waterfall in *The Last Salmon Run* had patterns just like the snow-covered mountains in the picture book. The gel pens allowed them to smoothly make lines over and over, which was easy on their handgrips.

We Are ArtMakers! Share and Communicate with Gel Pens

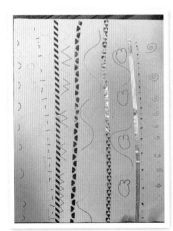 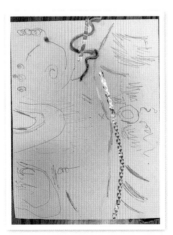

Children summarized that they could use their new knowledge to make lines, including patterns, to create detailed landscapes that express a certain mood.

"This is the sky, the wind, and the snow falling down because it is so cold. These are the lines for the sky when it is sunset. This is the water calm. This is the part of the sea. See the waves? Here are the fish. These are the octopus, and these are the swirls that are bubbles. The bottom is the sand. This is my sea, and I want people to feel calm and relaxed." —Clara, age six

"I made an ocean. There is seaweed and coral. I added shells and bubbles. I used circle patterns and repeated spikes. People will feel calm because this is an ocean with green and blue calming colors." —Locke, age six

Going Deeper with ArtMaking

Use this QR code or type www.redleafpress.org /amk/3-3.pdf into your browser to Go Deeper.

SYNTHESIZING OUR LEARNING ABOUT LINES

The children studied vertical, horizontal, diagonal, and organic lines and learned how they can make letters, numbers, and even art. They had first noticed lines in the book *In a Jar* by Deborah Marcero, and when we returned to this book to reflect and summarize all they had learned about lines, they loved the golden tones and noticed a new type of line. Therefore, we designed a new art makerspace to invite the children to use gold markers to create a final art installation to celebrate our learning.

While tinkering with the sequins and gold markers, they became curious about the images in Gustav Klimt's *Tree of Life* painting. They loved the look of the artwork and the gold markers, so we agreed to make a large mural together. Before making lines on paper, they wanted to practice making the large spirals together. We decided to gather the leaves falling all around us.

We brought the leaves back to begin playing and tinkering with spiral lines. The children curved the lines as they went to make a beautiful spiral maze.

After walking our spiral and playing with the lines, it was time to create the large mural. The children added their own spirals and began noticing and adding shapes they identified in the artwork, which became a great bridge to our next unit . . . shapes! The mural took several days to complete and became a special place to communicate all the things we were grateful for in our lives.

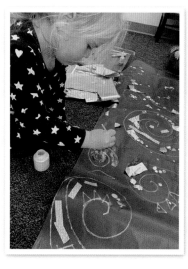

"My circles are tangled in a blanket of warm colors." Children combine their knowledge of colors and lines with an exploration of shapes. We discover the beauty in shapes, connect to mathematical geometric concepts in learning shapes, and witness the complex thinking of our children as they notice and observe, play and tinker, make and connect, and communicate their own thinking with shapes in their art.

Chapter 4

Making Meaning with Shapes

We select shapes as the next element of art to study, as children naturally begin to join their lines together to form geometric and organic shapes. As Obaleye Joseph Oludare and colleagues explain, "Shapes are significant in everyday life and the foundation for the comprehension of the natural and built environment" (2020, 765). Geometric shapes can be found in buildings and structures, while organic shapes are represented in the natural environment. Through our investigation of shapes, children learn they can apply their math lessons to their ArtMaking to help them better communicate their thinking. Transferring their knowledge from playing and tinkering with three-dimensional shapes (blocks, Magna-Tiles, window blocks) to two-dimensional shapes in their drawing and painting is a step toward developing their capabilities for more abstract thinking and representation.

As our young children learn to represent their thinking using the language of art, they learn how to break down objects into basic shapes. Instead of noticing a table or a tree, they begin to see squares, circles, triangles, and organic shapes, and they use these shapes to add clarity, emotion, movement, symmetry, and balance to their art. Children also add these shapes to their knowledge of lines as they gain proficiency with writing alphabetic letters. This continuum, represented in a series of documentation stories throughout the chapter, is meant to guide you as you begin planning your own shape invitations.

The preassessment is an invitation to explore all shapes to see where the children are with their understanding and uses of shapes in communicating movement, big ideas, emotions, settings, characters, and thinking. We recommend introducing loose parts you haven't used before that can be bent, folded, and "shaped" to engage imaginations and curiosities about shapes. Notice which children are familiar with both geometric and organic shapes; which children understand what happens when they join shapes together, take them apart, stack them, or flip them; and which children can articulate the manipulations of the shapes and use appropriate vocabulary.

Research suggests we develop visual literacy skills in young children using their background knowledge, linking familiar concepts of colors, lines, and shapes to what they already know and recognize in images. Therefore, we start with the most familiar shapes (Lopatovska et al. 2016; Pelo 2017). The first shape children typically start drawing is the circle. Playing with circles, dots, and ovals provides a continued focus on letter formation and also shows children how they can manipulate a basic shape (the circle) to make it more closely resemble their thinking. As they wonder about round shapes, they practice asking and answering questions, along with inferring the meaning of shape-shifting (dots to circles to ovals) in art. Next we introduce geometric shapes with straight lines. We first work with squares and rectangles, modeling how they work together

A Continuum of Shapes							
Setting the Stage	Circles	Dots and Ovals	Squares and Rectangles	Triangles	All Geometric Shapes	Organic Shapes	Symmetry

Setting the Stage

Circles

Dots and Ovals

Squares and Rectangles

Triangles

All Geometric Shapes

Organic Shapes

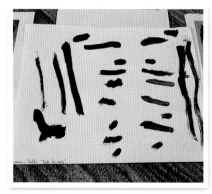

Symmetry

or separately and using them to represent places, actions, moods, and big ideas. We then discuss and study triangles (equilateral, acute, obtuse) and the many ways children can use triangles to represent things (on top of one another, conjoined at the base, tip to tip).

After a review of the shapes we've learned, we introduce organic shapes. Organic shapes are typically associated with nature, landscapes, and naturally occurring objects. They tend to represent things that grow, flow, and move (waves, plants). Organic shapes are more difficult for children to grasp, as they are more abstract and do not have conventional "rules" to follow in drawing them. Once the children have developed fluency with both geometric and organic shapes, they put their knowledge together with the more complex concept of symmetry and balance. They have fun trying out a new medium (traditional Chinese ink) as they learn about symmetry. Finally, our culminating inquiry combines all sorts of shapes (geometric and organic) as children enact their aesthetic sensibilities and make their version of beauty with shapes.

MAKING MEANING WITH AN INFORMAL PREASSESSMENT

The room transformed once more as we transitioned from our study of lines to our study of shapes. We placed translucent shapes on a light box as a tabletop provocation and incorporated shapes as loose parts in other areas in the room to provoke curiosity and excitement. To assess children's prior knowledge of shapes, we invited them to explore an art makerspace that prompted them to notice a variety of shapes, infer the meaning of how the shapes were being used to create images, and begin building vocabulary about geometry together.

Getting Ready for ArtMaking

During the first read of *Walter's Wonderful Web* by Tim Hopgood, the children discussed events through the book. They made text-to-self connections by sharing their personal experiences: "I saw a spiderweb before on a hike" and "I ran into a spiderweb one time and it made it fall down." To immerse the children in the aesthetics, we invited them to notice the lines and shapes from the illustrations. As they explored what they could make using crayons and markers, we could hear them commenting, "Look at his beautiful web!" and "The moon looks so big and pretty."

 Use this QR code or type www.redleafpress.org/amk/4-t.pdf into your browser to view the chart online; or find the chart in the appendix on page 164.

We Are Readers! Observe and Imagine using *Walter's Wonderful Web*

The engaging illustrations in *Walter's Wonderful Web* drew children into noticing new shapes. The last illustration of the book, with its beautiful and intricate display of shapes woven into the web, was ideal to launch our unit and assess prior knowledge. It provoked the children to look carefully and hunt for the tiny details in the image. They first noticed all the lines they had just learned from our line study. "There is a curved line." "Those lines are crisscross." "I see wavy lines." But it wasn't until one child saw the moon that our conversation shifted to seeing shapes. "I see a big bright moon." "What shape should we call this?" we asked. "That's a circle!" they shouted. Then they looked at the illustration with new eyes to hunt for other shapes.

We then invited children to imagine what they could draw with shapes using crayons, Flair pens, and Sharpie markers. The children were confident in creating lines but were very hesitant to try making shapes. We allowed plenty of time to try out the new Sharpie markers and to inquire about how they would use and incorporate shapes into their art.

We Are Makers! Play and Tinker with Yarn and Translucent Shapes

After returning to the illustration from *Walter's Wonderful Web*, the children began to think more deeply about the picture and infer its meaning. The children agreed the main message was that Walter created something beautiful because he never gave up.

The children used yarn to represent their own web line patterns and were curious to try the shapes as well. They started layering shapes across the yarn. Then we noticed children tinkering with only the shapes by assembling the pieces as if making a collage. They were beginning to understand that everything has shapes that can be put together to draw pictures.

We Are Artists! Connect and Make with Alexander Calder

We invited the children to view *Quilt*, a painting by Alexander Calder. Calder was known mostly for his mobiles (sculptures), but his paintings show his explorations of movement and shapes.

The children immediately began making text-to-text connections to the same shapes in the book illustration. "They both made circles." "This shape is here and here too," another child said, referring to the rectangle. We were assessing which shapes and geometry vocabulary were still unknown and what instruction we needed to provide in drawing shapes.

We Are ArtMakers! Share and Communicate with Crayons, Flair Pens, and Sharpie Markers

We explored big ideas found in the artworks, as paintings and "illustrations always have to be about something" (Bryan 2019, 11). Each child summarized their learning by naming their big ideas.

"I made a unicorn. The big idea is that just because you don't see a unicorn doesn't mean it is not alive."
—Madelyn, age four

"I made a den for a dragon and wolves. The big idea is that we can all be happy together." —Reed, age four

"It really looks like a real dragon! I put the shapes on top of each other to make the head, body, and tail. Shapes can help you make the picture you want to draw." —Cole, age six

ArtMaking Tip

To build our youngest ArtMakers' confidence, it helps to model how to trace shapes.

MAKING MEANING WITH CIRCLES

The first investigation into shapes was circles because, as we stated in *Makerspaces*, "circles are one of the first shapes that children experiment with" (54). We designed tabletop and other provocations around the room to build curios-

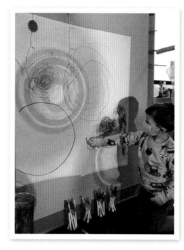

ity and wonder. "Look how big I made the circle!" and "Let's try adding the blue one" were some of the shouts we heard as the children played with light. "Look at all the moon shapes," one child called out as they began to explore the tray of circular loose parts that reminded them of the night sky and the moon from the previous book.

Inspiration for Making Meaning	Materials for Making Meaning
• Book: *Here We Are* by Oliver Jeffers • Art: *Several Circles, 1926* by Wassily Kandinsky	• Loose parts: Circular metal and glass pieces • Main material: Black construction and scrapbook paper • Medium: Chalk pastels

We Are Readers! Observe and Imagine with *Here We Are*

The first read aloud of *Here We Are* by Oliver Jeffers resulted in many connections: "That's Earth!" "That's the ocean." "There is a mountain." We zoomed in and used our visual literacy skills to analyze the illustration that generated the most questions.

This illustration layers circles together to represent the thinking brain of a child, which the children did not recognize at first. As we lingered with the image, the children began to retell everything they remembered seeing. They recognized common items such as lines, circles, toys, the sun, and the moon right away. We asked, "Why are these objects floating around?" One child said, "It's in her head! She's thinking!" This realization let us go deeper with our comprehension skills by infer-ring what was really happening in the illustration. The children agreed that the main idea was "We all have heads full of questions, and our heads are for thinking." They realized that shapes were used to show us all the questions the person was thinking about.

We Are Makers! Play and Tinker with Circular Reflective Loose Parts

We modeled moving jar lids, binder rings, and glass gems on a black circle base to show how you can tinker, layer, and change until you capture the image you want. We encouraged the children to re-create the circles with chalk pastels on another piece of black construction paper.

ArtMaking Tip

We recommend providing a paper base for children to tinker with loose parts and keep the materials together so they can refer to the image as they re-create it with the art medium. Here we provided children with black paper circles to hold their ideas.

We Are Artists! Connect and Make with Wassily Kandinsky

We returned to the artist Wassily Kandinsky with a very different painting from before. Kandinsky believed the circle was a complex shape with many ideas captured in it. The children immediately made text-to-text connections between the circles in both works of art. Children shared that Kandinsky's *Several Circles* looked like planets floating in space, a bunch of eyeballs, and even confetti at a birthday party. We discussed the mood, and they determined that Kandinsky used colors and circles to show his imagination.

"He used lots of dots that feel like a party." The children remembered that art can communicate a mood: "He used blue and green that makes me feel happy and calm."

We Are ArtMakers! Share and Communicate with Chalk Pastels

The children summarized their learning by using circles to express their thoughts, memories, favorite places, movement, creatures, and moods.

LEFT: Blair points to the blue circles in her artwork to communicate a waterfall she saw with her parents: "I made my family. We went on a big waterfall, and it was very cold that day. The mood is happy because people always feel happy when they see waterfalls." —Blair, age four

RIGHT: Fleur completes her circles using chalk pastels and shares her intent to make people feel excitement. She synthesized that shapes can be used to represent a feeling or emotion: "This is about people seeing fireworks at night. They are exciting and pretty to watch." —Fleur, age four

MAKING MEANING WITH DOTS, OVALS, AND OBLONG SHAPES

Once children have developed fluency with making circles, they can experiment with manipulating circles to create new versions, including dots, ovals, and oblong shapes, to better represent their thinking. We invited the children to play with light using transparent colored bowls along with plastic bracelets to project, move, and layer circle shapes. The tabletop invitations were inspired by Yayoi Kusama. The children placed dot stickers in a small world makerspace and on lanterns that would hang in our dot-covered space.

ArtMaking Tip

Museums offer photographs of paintings in their collections and videos of people visiting their art installations. The children watched visitors at the Tate Britain Museum cover a white room in dot stickers just like they were covering their small world makerspace with dot stickers. The children had no idea that this is one of Yayoi Kusama's obliteration rooms, but they were in awe, asking questions about where this was and what the people were making.

Inspiration for Making Meaning	Materials for Making Meaning
• Book: *Mae among the Stars* by Roda Ahmed, illustrated by Stasia Burrington • Art: *Stars and Pollen* by Yayoi Kusama	• Loose parts: Transparent plastic cut in circular shapes • Main material: White copy paper • Medium: Markers, dot markers

We Are Readers! Observe and Imagine with *Mae among the Stars*

We read *Mae among the Stars* by Roda Ahmed. Stasia Burrington's illustrations offered many circular shapes in the oblong and oval star-studded sky. The children pointed out all the circles across the night sky as well as the shape of planet Earth and even circles on the blanket.

We Are Makers! Play and Tinker with Transparent Circular Loose Parts

We returned to the book illustration, and the children inferred that the little girl was dreaming about going to space. They were amazed that this story was about a real little girl, Mae Jemison, who followed her dreams and became an astronaut! We modeled tinkering with circular loose parts and then showed how to stamp with dot markers and draw ovals and circles with markers. I thought out loud, "I wonder what this could be?" and "Where could I add more circles and ovals?" and then shared my idea, "This is starting to look like a pond. Maybe I want to dream of going to a pond."

The children wanted to make circles and ovals too, so they used circular loose parts along with markers and dot markers. They found other circles in the classroom, such as the bubble timers, and brought them to the art makerspace.

We Are Artists! Connect and Make with Yayoi Kusama

The children then learned about the Japanese artist Yayoi Kusama. They were fascinated by her style and all the dot and circle art she created. Kusama used her imagination to color her world with round shapes, using nature as her main inspiration.

The children made text-to-text connections that the illustration from *Mae among the Stars* and the artwork from Kusama both were about dreaming and creating joy.

And just as Kusama created rooms of dots for people to dream and feel joy and happiness, the children began filling our room up with dots, circles, and ovals too.

We Are ArtMakers! Share and Communicate with Dot Markers and Markers

We collected all the artifacts and artwork to make a documentation panel to celebrate and summarize our learning about circles, dots, and ovals. The children learned that they could use circles, dots, and ovals to create settings, moods, and actions.

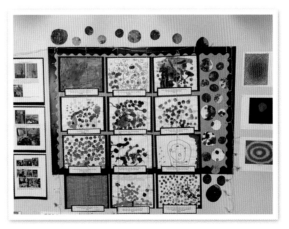

"I made a playground. I want people to know you can play on it and it will make you feel happy."
—Joshua, age four (upper right corner).

"I made a beach. They can go swimming and build sandcastles, which will make them feel happy." —Fleur, age four (last row, middle).

Going Deeper with ArtMaking

Use this QR code or type www.redleafpress.org/amk/4-1.pdf into your browser to Go Deeper.

MAKING MEANING WITH SQUARES AND RECTANGLES

Next we investigated the square and rectangle. The children immediately recognized that these shapes were made of straight lines, and some children were able to name the shapes. We encouraged children who weren't ready to draw these shapes independently to use the loose parts for models or for tracing, but most of all for playing and tinkering!

Inspiration for Making Meaning	Materials for Making Meaning
• Book: *Finding Wild* by Megan Wagner Lloyd, illustrated by Abigail Halpin • Art: *Six Prisons* and *Orange Prison* by Peter Halley	• Loose parts: Window blocks, Magna-Tiles, and washi tape • Main material: White paper, canvas • Medium: Tempera paint sticks

We Are Readers! Observe and Imagine with *Finding Wild*

Our investigation into squares and rectangles started by enjoying *Finding Wild* by Megan Wagner Lloyd. The following day, we zoomed in on the illustration of the city scene. Illustrator Abigail Halpin used lines, squares, and rectangles to make a busy city spring to life on the page. Children studied the illustration and retold everything they saw. They brought forward their knowledge of lines and began to see shapes, like circles and squares, on the buildings.

Furthering their understanding that illustrations can hold many meanings, each child inferred what was happening in the image and used text evidence to support their thinking. For example, when a child noticed the leaf in the illustration, she inferred, "It is windy because the leaf is following the path."

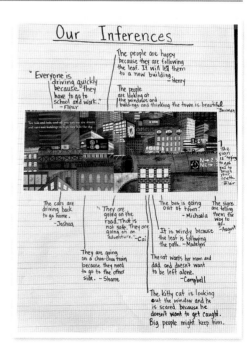

We Are Makers! Play and Tinker with Window Blocks, Magna-Tiles, and Washi Tape

Inspired by our read-aloud book, the children tinkered with loose parts to imagine what they could make with squares and rectangles. They created towers of buildings and used washi tape to add lines for windows. They also created presents and used washi tape as ribbons.

We Are Artists! Connect and Make with Peter Halley

Then the children were ready to meet Peter Halley and his art. They made text-to-text connections between his rectangular and square art and the city scene from *Finding Wild*. We learned that Halley made these paintings when he moved to New York City and found people alone and separate in their apartments. But as time went on, he used bright colors to represent the life and busyness he felt in the city. The children then each developed ideas about a big idea or mood they could make.

They returned to the art makerspace and used tempera paint sticks in neon colors just like Halley. The squares and rectangles were full of powerful messages!

We Are Makers! Play and Tinker with Mosaic Triangles

The following day, we asked the children, "What do you think is happening in the illustration?" and "What do you think the illustrator wants us to understand about his illustration?" Below are their inferences on the big idea.

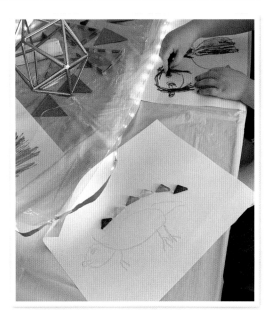

> "Beekle is trying to find a friend. You can always find a new friend." —August, age three

> "You can go wherever you want to find new toys to play with." —Bowman, age four

> "Follow and you will find a mystery." —Cai, age four

> "The cloud sees that he does not have a friend. We all need friends." —Fleur, age four

> "You can have fun at any place, like the playground or the park." —Joshua, age four

> "You can find things." —Campbell Grace, age three

> "He is following the dots." —Shane, age three

After the focus lesson, the children tinkered with the triangle loose parts before and while drawing with oil pastels. Some children were inspired to make scales for a dinosaur while others made patterns with the mosaic tiles prior to drawing their new ideas.

We Are Artists! Connect and Make with Jean-Michel Basquiat

Next we introduced the children to Jean-Michel Basquiat. Santat's illustrations complemented the crown icon seen throughout Basquiat's artwork. The children enjoyed learning about graffiti, as he was first a graffiti artist who became a painter. They learned about the artist by listening to *Radiant Child* by Javaka Steptoe. We displayed many pieces of his art in the art makerspace. They noticed the crown showing up again and again and made text-to-text connections to Beekle's crown made of triangles. Their favorite was the dinosaur with the crown in *Pez Dispenser*, and they inferred that this means we should "make our own friends" and "always have fun."

We Are ArtMakers! Share and Communicate with Oil Pastels

More and more, the children were synthesizing their learning by using their knowledge from previous investigations (color and lines) as well as from our previous studies of shapes (circles, squares, rectangles) to communicate meaning.

Shane recalled the illustration of Beekle following the dotted line to find his new friend. Shane synthesized this learning and made his own version: "I made a path. It means you should follow." —Shane, age three

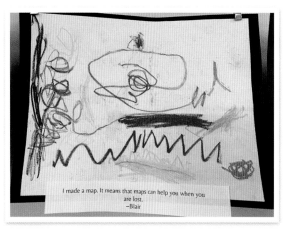

Blair noticed how Beekle followed the dotted line as well and created a map to symbolize how he was searching for a friend and how he worried that he would not find who he was looking for. "Maps can help you when you're lost." —Blair, age four

MAKING MEANING WITH ALL GEOMETRIC SHAPES

The next investigation was a perfect opportunity to linger with all the geometric shapes we had learned in both math and ArtMaking, before moving on to organic shapes. We invited the children to build with wooden blocks, wooden shapes they had painted at another tabletop provocation, and wooden craft sticks to reinforce making with circles, ovals, squares, rectangles, and triangles. We also laid out cardboard shapes and other recycled materials to glue together. The cardboard mural became an ongoing invitation to continue adding shapes and color throughout the investigation.

Inspiration for Making Meaning	Materials for Making Meaning
• Book: *Home* by Carson Ellis • Art: Disney artwork by Mary Blair, starting with *South American Goodwill Tour*	• Loose parts: Wooden blocks and Popsicle sticks • Main material: White paper • Medium: Tempera paint cakes • Tools: Brushes

We Are Readers! Observe and Imagine with *Home*

As the children listened to *Home* by Carson Ellis, they were fascinated with the different types of homes and wondered who lived there.

The illustration they wondered about most was the dome-like home that asked the question, "Who in the world lives here?" The home contained many of the shapes we had been investigating.

It also introduced a rhombus and hinted at some organic shapes. The children instantly connected to their background knowledge of shapes (big and little circles, rectangular door, triangle cave) and used their retelling skills to recall what they noticed: steam out of pipe, stairs leading to nowhere. We invited the children to use the wooden loose parts again but this time asked them to imagine what they could build and then draw with tempera paint cakes.

We Are Makers! Play and Tinker with Wood Pieces

The following day, we revisited the illustration and began discussing the children's inferences to find a deeper meaning in their observations. They used the text evidence to support their ideas: "This is a home on another planet." "The bubble is protecting them from the outside." "Look at the planets and stars in the sky. This is another world." The children began making more complex structures by weaving Popsicle sticks into their design.

We Are Artists! Connect and Make with Mary Blair

We were excited to introduce the children to Mary Blair, with the many brightly colored and geometric spaces in her art, as well as her famous *It's a Small World* design for Disneyland. Blair used her colors and shapes to tell stories and portray emotions. The children made text-to-text connections using the many geometric shapes in each artwork and took this inspiration to the art makerspace to consider the loose parts and mediums with new purpose.

We Are ArtMakers! Share and Communicate with Tempera Paint Cakes

After studying Blair's art for inspiration, the children continued adding layers of bright paint and geometric shapes to their cardboard mural to summarize their learning. They expressed that it was important to learn these shapes because then they could draw more than one shape to create different settings and favorite places. For example, a square becomes a house and a triangle a roof. Together we created a documentation panel to summarize what we had learned so far. Then they synthesized their learning by sharing their creations.

"I made a lemonade tree growing high. There is grass growing. I drew circles to show that grapes were growing on it. There are circle planets and a helicopter flying. I want people to feel happy about this amazing place." —Blair, age four (top left).

"I made a home with rectangles and squares on another planet. I want people to feel safe here." —Michaela, age four (third row, right).

ArtMaking Tip

Consider introducing the principles of combining straight and diagonal lines with other angles to make stars, pentagons, hexagons, and so on. The Kinderoo Children's Academy designed provocations for children to make interesting shapes, inspired by Frida Kahlo's use of shapes in her artwork.

Going Deeper with ArtMaking

Use this QR code or type www.redleafpress.org /amk/4-2.pdf into your browser to Go Deeper.

MAKING MEANING WITH ORGANIC SHAPES

Organic shapes inspired by nature filled the room: projections of images, transparency cutouts on the light table, and the tabletop invitation for children to combine fabric pieces, nature loose parts, and wooden puzzle blocks. Organic shapes tend to represent things that grow, flow, and move, and they give children permission and freedom to create their own shapes. They use their foundational knowledge of the formation and intention of geometric shapes while learning they can create their own shapes to better represent their thinking and feelings in their art.

To launch this investigation, one prekindergarten classroom of four- and five-year-olds created a chart to summarize what they had learned about geometric shapes, to introduce how organic shapes are different, and to make connections to their everyday lives so they could relate to the new content.

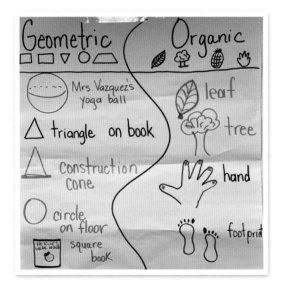

Inspiration for Making Meaning	Materials for Making Meaning
• Book: *If I Had a Little Dream* by Nina Laden, illustrated by Melissa Castrillon • Art: *The Ten Largest* by Hilma af Klint	• Loose parts: Fabric pieces, wooden cookies, and organic shape block puzzles • Main material: White construction paper • Medium: Watercolor paints • Tools: Cups for water, thin brushes

We Are Readers! Observe and Imagine with *If I Had a Little Dream*

The children were immediately drawn into the whimsical illustrations and oversized world that illustrator Melissa Castrillon had created. We chose this book because it represents the organic shapes we find outside and then invites us to make up new plants and places using these shapes. When we returned to zoom in on an illustration, the children immediately saw the small house, leaves, flowers, birds, and other animals and insects. Then one noticed that "the trees are full of air." After the focus lesson, they tried organic shapes for the first time using new neon watercolors and brushes.

We Are Makers! Play and Tinker with Fabric and Wooden Loose Parts

The children were curious about the new watercolor brush markers, so a quick demonstration was all they needed before starting to tinker with organic shapes. They were encouraged to build with wooden and fabric loose parts and then keep the construction so they could refer to it as they painted.

ArtMaking Tip

Nature offers a wealth of loose parts in organic shapes. This group of prekindergarten four- and five-year-olds tinkered with the organic shapes of rocks, leaves, feathers, shells, and sticks before drawing them on paper.

We Are Artists! Connect and Make with Hilma af Klint

We then showed the children artwork from Hilma af Klint, who painted organic shapes from her imagination. Art from *The Ten Largest* exhibit connected strongly to the nature-inspired organic shapes the children loved in the book. They made text-to-text connections that many shapes in Klint's art looked like the flowers, petals, seeds, and plants from the book. The children were inspired to create new places, both imaginary and real-life worlds.

We Are ArtMakers! Share and Communicate with Watercolor Brush Markers and Paint

For most of the children, the concept of organic shapes was new, but they used their knowledge from previous studies to combine the organic shapes with colors, lines, and geometric shapes. Their words indicated their understanding that organic shapes can create moods, movement, and even the whole world.

"This is a trail where we are going. Follow and you can be happy." —Blair, age four

Reed, age four, synthesized her understanding that it is important to learn how to draw organic shapes because you can create your own places. She shared that she made a trap for leprechauns to find their treasure.

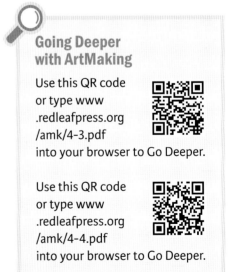

Going Deeper with ArtMaking

Use this QR code or type www .redleafpress.org /amk/4-3.pdf into your browser to Go Deeper.

Use this QR code or type www .redleafpress.org /amk/4-4.pdf into your browser to Go Deeper.

MAKING MEANING WITH SYMMETRY

Symmetry is an important concept in the shape study because many shapes are symmetrical. An investigation into symmetry deepens children's knowledge of shapes, inviting them to figure out ways to divide them evenly in half. Symmetry is also our introduction to balance in art. So our next step was to inspire children to see symmetry in art, understand what meanings it can hold, and consider how they can re-create it in their own ArtMaking.

Inspiration for Making Meaning	Materials for Making Meaning
• Book: *Shadow* by Suzy Lee • Art: *94 Fish* by M. C. Escher	• Loose parts: Nature materials (leaves, flowers, wood cookies), shadows • Main material: Black and white construction paper • Medium: Traditional Chinese ink • Tools: Bamboo brushes, washi tape, ice cube trays

We are Readers! Observe and Imagine with *Shadow*

The children had curious looks as they listened to *Shadow* by Suzy Lee, actively scanning the pages to understand the illustrations. Both the children and I as their educator were using all the visual clues in this wordless picture book to interpret and communicate the story. We loved the illustrations because at the beginning, the objects' shadows showcase symmetry. As the story continues, the illustrations of the shadows help children imagine what they can make when they play with shadows on paper.

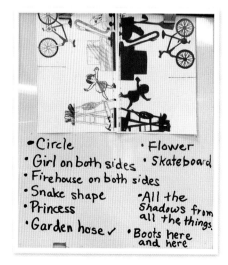

When the children zoomed in on the most symmetrical illustration in the book, they noticed the clearly seen objects (flower, skateboard, garden hose) while making connections to their shape knowledge (circles on bike). Then they began noticing how the objects were the same on both sides. "Fire hose is on both sides." "Boots are here and here." They were noticing symmetry and ready to explore the concept using traditional Chinese black ink.

We Are Makers! Play and Tinker with Loose Parts

We revisited the book the next day to use our inferring skills. The children expressed big ideas: "You can pretend with shadows" and "You can make shadows come to life." They made a collaborative collage by choosing a nature loose part to place on one side of a line and then selecting a matching object to place on the other side of the line that we placed on the carpet. Then they looked throughout the learning space for loose parts to tinker with symmetry, finding pom-poms, Lego bricks, flowers, magnetic blocks, and other open-ended materials. Introducing this concept with loose parts affirmed that exploration leads to new learning.

We Are Artists! Connect and Make with M. C. Escher

With a stronger understanding of symmetry, we engaged in a collaborative ArtMaking experience to encourage making purposeful marks instead of filling the page with ink. We used washi tape on a large piece of paper as the center line. We painted one style of a line on one side of the tape and then invited a child to use their knowledge of symmetry to make the same stroke on the other side of the tape. This solidified their understanding of symmetry and led us to M. C. Escher. Much of his work is the result of mathematical investigations. The children loved the repetition of the designs in black and white and noticed fish, salamanders, and birds. Then we invited the children to return to the art makerspace, now with a deeper understanding of symmetrical designs.

We Are ArtMakers! Share and Communicate with Traditional Chinese Ink

Children were learning that art can convey an intentional message. When asked, "What is the message/meaning of your artwork?" they had a lot to say!

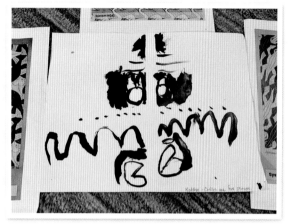

Madelyn, age four, made a castle and shared that "castles are for princesses."

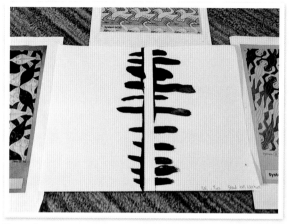

"I made a tree. It means that you can stand tall like trees." —Cai, age four

SYNTHESIZING OUR LEARNING ABOUT SHAPES

To synthesize all we had learned during the shapes study and to inspire a collaborative art piece to summarize and apply our new ArtMaking skills, we set up a small world makerspace for children to

play with shapes and light. We read *A River* by Marc Martin, and the illustrations combined children's knowledge of geometric shapes (in the city scenes) and organic shapes (in the jungle scenes).

We zoomed in on the jungle illustration with the river flowing through, and the children observed plants, flowers, trees, water, birds, and other animals hiding in the lush forest. With their investigation of organic shapes still fresh on their minds, they concentrated on identifying these shapes in the leaves. They also used their background knowledge from earlier studies to discuss the lines on the leaves and stems and the eyes peeking through as circles. Over the next few days, they shared some big ideas from the illustration and what these shapes meant to them. "The trees are swaying and making beautiful music," one child expressed, explaining their understanding that shapes could be used to show movement and demonstrate a mood. "The stream is moving to another building and place," chimed in another, sharing that the character in the book was on an adventure and explaining that we can make stories and art that are our own adventure ideas as well.

They were then invited to play and tinker in the art makerspace to combine geometric and organic shapes using pencils, watercolors, and tempera paint cakes from the study. A lot of children had learned to trace shapes to make them confidently and then fill in the space with color.

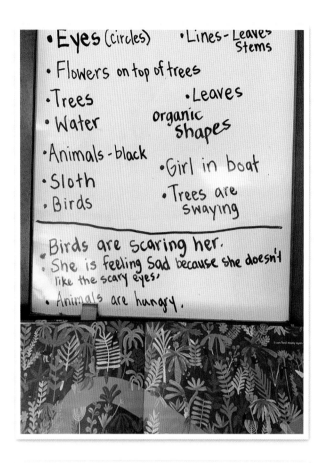

After a few days of tinkering with shapes, we introduced the children to several pieces by Henri Matisse (*The Parakeet and the Mermaid, Composition noir et rouge, Composition fond vert*). These works were cutouts, and Matisse's process has been called painting with scissors. We listened to the story *Matisse's Garden* by Samantha Friedman, and the children made text-to-text connections between the shapes they saw in the picture book and in Matisse's pieces. We suggested that we could make a large mural together that looked just like Matisse's art, using shapes.

The children were excited as we gathered around a large piece of white bulletin board paper to discuss our design, tracing or drawing geometric and organic shapes with black Sharpies.

When the mural was bursting with shapes, it was time to add color. We continued to read books about Matisse, and they loved his bright colors. Therefore, we provided neon watercolors and tempera paint cakes for the children to add vibrant beauty to their mural.

Before the mural was complete, the children recalled how Matisse added cutout pieces of paper shapes to his art, and they wanted to use the same technique. They gathered the remaining pieces of the paper cutouts and glued them on to complete the mural. With the finished art displayed on the wall, we reflected on what we had learned about shapes and discussed what we should call our art. One child said, "It's our own garden!" "It's like we are all being friends in our garden," another child added. In the end, the children synthesized their understanding of shapes by making something new: their friendship garden. They worked together making geometric and organic shapes to create something beautiful and meaningful that they will always remember. Making friends. Working together. ArtMaking!

"This is a dragon that lives in outer space. The dragon feels fuzzy. This place feels joy."
Children discover textures as they explore their worlds with their senses. Textures can
add details as ArtMakers communicate their thinking.

Chapter 5

Making Meaning with Textures

Texture is ubiquitous and a significant part of the sensory input we receive every day, aligning to what young children are learning in science as they use their senses to explore and understand their worlds. In the visual arts, texture is the real or perceived surface quality of a work of art. Even when children cannot feel the texture in a painting, they can see the intentional use of colors (shiny, smooth), lines (prickly, feathery, furry), and shapes (bumpy, rough, sharp).

Texture is the next element of art in our study. Once children have developed fluency with colors, lines, and shapes, the next step is to elaborate their ArtMaking with textural details. Texture in illustrations cannot be felt by touch but instead represents the feeling of a surface (Liu, Lughofer, and Zeng 2015). Children can better represent their thinking by adding texture to their language of art. We use loose parts with real textures to scaffold our young artists in learning to imply these textures in their art, building on their previous knowledge of colors, lines, and shapes. We can integrate science concepts and use touch to learn about the world. Noticing and making textures increases children's understanding of their senses. They use sight to discover how artists use the art elements to represent textures and touch to explore the textures of loose parts.

This continuum, represented in a series of documentation stories throughout the chapter, is meant to guide you as you begin planning your own texture invitation.

The preassessment is an invitation to explore many textures; to determine what children already know, including how they use texture-related vocabulary and how they use textures to add details; and to better scaffold their learning in this unit. As we often layer mediums to imply textures, we recommend introducing several mediums to see which textures children are familiar with, which are most intriguing to the children, and which will need explicit modeling and instruction.

Each learning engagement serves as a review of an art element the children have already used and then adds texture as a layered detail (such as using circles and dots to add bumpy textures). Using multiple mediums together adds layers, highlights, and complexity. We start by showing how to use light and dark colors to represent a smooth and shiny surface. This reviews what children already know about color while teaching them to better represent smooth and shiny objects in their art. Noticing subtleties in colors improves their observational skills and adds to their descriptive language. We then move to lines, using straight and angled lines to show prickly and spiky textures, weighted lines to show feathery textures, and contoured lines to show scaly textures. As we increase complexity, we review shapes: squares and rectangles can show rough surfaces (brick walls, stone paths, buildings), and triangles can imply sharp textures (teeth, pointed objects).

A Continuum of Textures								
Setting the stage	Smooth and Shiny	Prickly and Spiky	Feathery and Fluffy	Hairy and Furry	Scaly	Bumpy	Rough	Sharp

Setting the Stage

Using Light and Dark Colors
to Show Smooth and Shiny

Using Straight and Angled Lines
to Show Prickly and Spiky

Using Weighted Lines to Show
Feathery and Fluffy

Using Organic Lines to Show
Hairy and Furry

Using Contoured Lines
to Show Scaly

Using Circles and Dots
to Show Bumpy

Using Squares and Rectangles
to Show Rough

Using Triangles to Show Sharp

MAKING MEANING WITH AN INFORMAL PREASSESSMENT

To begin our study of textures, we designed a tabletop provocation that displayed items with a variety of textures (bark, nest, shells, snakeskin, feather, lace, sandpaper, rock) alongside magnifying glasses and a projector microscope. We encouraged the children to feel the loose parts and look closely at how the textures are made.

Getting Ready for ArtMaking

After the first read of *A Little Bit Brave* by Nicola Kinnear, the children discussed their favorite parts of the plot. They made text-to-self connections about their feelings and what they like, such as "I like going outside too, like the bunny." "I have felt nervous about going outside on a hike too." "Hikes are scary because of the thorns, and they make me tired." To immerse the children in the aesthetics of texture, we invited them to notice textures of real objects. They also lingered on their favorite illustration to enjoy the beauty and aesthetics, with comments like, "The bunny is soft and cute" and "The river looks wet and refreshing."

 Use this QR code or type www.redleafpress.org/amk /5-t.pdf into your browser to view the chart online, or find the chart in the appendix on page 165.

We Are Readers! Observe and Imagine with *A Little Bit Brave*

After reading *A Little Bit Brave* by Nicola Kinnear, we zoomed in on the illustration of the eagle spreading his wings, which captured a variety of natural textures. A child commented, "I see an otter. It feels soft."

We Are Makers! Play and Tinker with Loose Parts with Different Textures

The next day, we revisited the illustration to think more deeply about it. First we inferred the illustration's location. The children felt it was the woods because of the trees and animals. Then one child commented on the bunnies' facial expressions, which led us to talk about mood. The children all agreed the feeling was joy, using details in the illustration to back up their thinking. As children infer what they think and then use text evidence to support it, they develop strong thinking behaviors that create a foundation for reading. Children were then invited to explore textures in the art makerspace.

The children enjoyed making rubbings with shoe soles. They noticed that some textures, like fur, were difficult to capture with a crayon rubbing. They wondered how they could make textures like fur and hair, and this made them excited to learn more.

ArtMaking Tip

Flat crayons make better rubbings, so we took the paper off some of the crayons, and we also added Crayon Rocks, which are flat on one side. Simple prompts to place the objects under the paper helped the children explore the materials and notice the difference between actual texture and implied texture.

We Are Artists! Connect and Make with Martin Johnson Heade

We shared *Cattleya Orchid and Three Hummingbirds*, a painting by Martin Johnson Heade that provides a variety of textures. Heade captured his joy of nature with his attention to textured details. Some children inferred that the image evoked a scary mood because of the darker colors, while others inferred a magical mood, suggesting the scene could be a "fairy garden" or a "garden where birds live." Our conversations generated new understandings of how textures contribute to the mood and setting.

We Are ArtMakers! Share and Communicate with Crayons and Watercolors

Students explored textures to represent settings, characters, and moods.

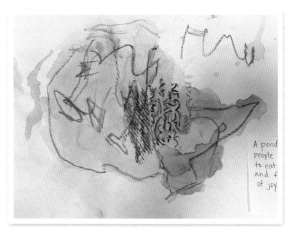

"This place is a tent where you can roast marshmallows on the fire. The tent makes you feel warm and snuggly." —Campbell Grace, age three

"This is a pond where people can go to eat worms and find lots of joy." —Bowman, age four

MAKING MEANING USING DARK AND LIGHT COLORS TO SHOW SMOOTH AND SHINY TEXTURES

We introduced a daily mystery box during this investigation, and it quickly became the most anticipated moment each day! Each child reached into the box and described what they felt. This built vocabulary and made connections to science concepts as we used our senses to learn about the world. We created a texture chart and labeled it with the children's descriptions of the mystery box contents (such as "shiny and smooth"). We taped a piece of the object next to the chart to help children remember the texture name.

We recommend a smooth texture as the first investigation because it uses light and dark color, the first element we studied, to achieve the implied texture. As we continue through the texture studies, we move through the continuum of art elements, again reinforcing and deepening the children's knowledge with the new purpose of making texture.

Inspiration for Making Meaning	Materials for Making Meaning
• Book: *Florette* by Anna Walker • Art: *Pineapple Bud* by Georgia O'Keeffe and *Heliconia, Crab's Claw Ginger*	• Loose parts: Shiny leaves and succulents • Main material: White construction paper • Medium: Tempera paint sticks

We Are Readers! Observe and Imagine with *Florette*

The children loved the plants in *Florette* and made text-to-self connections with the plants in the mystery box and outside our classroom doors. "That plant looks smooth like that one [pointing]!" We chose an illustration showing a variety of plants by Anna Walker because it showed smooth textures using light and dark greens, adding light and white color on top of darker colors.

We Are Makers! Play and Tinker with Succulents

After the children retold the details in the illustration, we discussed their inferences about what was happening. Many children appreciated the beauty of the place and thought people could go there and feel happy. The children then tinkered with the tempera paint sticks, layering colors to achieve a smooth texture. We provided single-stem succulents along with other natural and plastic loose parts that children could trace and tinker with on their page.

We Are Artists! Connect and Make with Georgia O'Keeffe

We introduced the children to *Pineapple Bud (1939)* and *Heliconia, Crab's Claw Ginger* by Georgia O'Keeffe. O'Keeffe is known for her textured details of nature. The children made text-to-text connections between O'Keeffe's art and all the green plants in *Florette*. We modeled how to draw the organic shapes of a green plant and then add white curved lines to make a smooth implied texture. We then invited the children to make their own with their new knowledge of texture making.

ArtMaking Tip

Many children love paint and want to keep adding layers. But even though they have fun adding layers, they can become disappointed when their original image or idea is accidentally covered up. To allow the process art to continue happening while still showcasing all they have learned, you can ask if they would like another piece of paper to continue their making.

We Are ArtMakers! Share and Communicate with Tempera Paint Sticks

As the children explored at length, they began using vocabulary associated with smooth textures.

"I made a garden full of smooth and soft flowers."
—Reed, age four

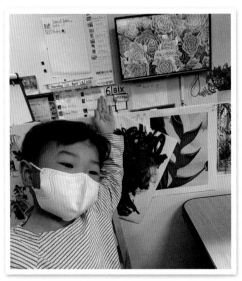

"I used red just like this smooth plant."
—Shane, age three

MAKING MEANING USING STRAIGHT AND ANGLED LINES TO SHOW PRICKLY AND SPIKY TEXTURES

Prickly and spiky texture was next in the continuum because it drew on children's previous knowledge of straight and angled lines. We projected book pages around the room to immerse children in the images and textures. In morning meeting, the mystery box contained woodland animal ornaments with hair made of wooden, spiky pieces.

Inspiration for Making Meaning	Materials for Making Meaning
• Book: *Wolfie the Bunny* by Ame Dyckman, illustrated by Zachariah OHora • Art: *Porcupines* by Robert Winthrop Chanler	• Loose parts: Toothpicks, beechnuts, wood sticks • Main material: White copy paper • Medium: Pencils and Sharpies • Tools: Overhead projector

We Are Readers! Observe and Imagine with *Wolfie the Bunny*

We selected *Wolfie the Bunny* by Ame Dyckman and illustrated by Zachariah OHora for the strong, noticeable lines that foreshadow upcoming textures, like rough bricks and a woven pattern. The children noticed the lines on the bunny and said that this was "spiky" texture.

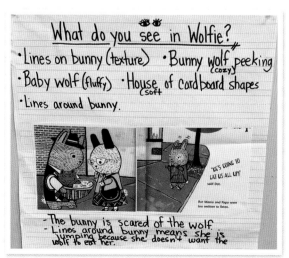

We Are Makers! Play and Tinker with Natural and Wooden Loose Parts

We then discussed what we saw happening in the illustration and modeled how to use loose parts to imagine a textured character. The children inferred that the bunny was "scared of the wolf," using text evidence to explain that the lines around the bunny meant she was jumping and moving because she was afraid the wolf would eat her. Children tinkered with placing toothpicks on felt animals and organic shapes to help them imagine how and where to add spiky texture.

We Are Artists! Connect and Make with Robert Winthrop Chanler

The children watched a *Ready, Set, Draw!* video of OHora demonstrating how he drew short lines to imply texture, and they drew along with him. This experience scaffolded their understanding of texture and gave them confidence in making their own textured characters.

We then introduced the children to *Porcupine* by Robert Winthrop Chanler. They made text-to-text connections between it and the *Wolfie the Bunny* illustration, as both images represented a family and had spiky texture because of the lines. They explained that the porcupines were scared like the bunny because it looked like "they were stuck in the mud."

We Are ArtMakers! Share and Communicate with Pencils and Sharpies

The children made spiky and prickly characters, using the visual language of art to develop a deep understanding of who their characters are and what they look like. The children wanted to add their characters to the places they made while studying smooth texture, so we cut the characters out so they could glue them on. The children incorporated their new texture vocabulary as they summarized their artworks.

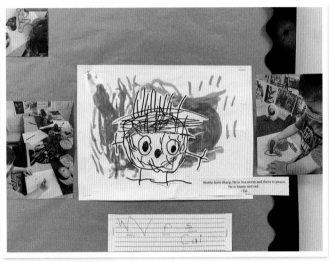

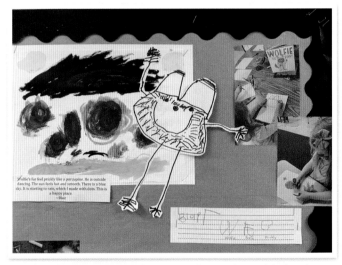

"Wolfie feels sharp. He is in a storm and there is peace. He is happy and sad." —Cai, age four

"Wolfie's fur feels prickly like a porcupine. He is outside dancing. The sun feels hot and smooth. There is a blue sky. It is starting to rain, which I made with dots. This is a happy place." —Blair, age four

ArtMaking Tip

Try holding a museum walk to summarize and celebrate learning at the end of an investigation. Display all the art on a table or walls and allow the children to walk around and share what they notice. Older children can use sticky notes to leave comments for the ArtMaker.

MAKING MEANING USING WEIGHTED LINES TO SHOW FEATHERY TEXTURES

The next investigation connected back to our line study, using weighted lines (thick and thin) to create feathery textures. A table-top provocation invited children to explore feathers using the magnifying glass and projectable microscope. We also projected the book page from *The Day I Became a Bird* that showcased a variety of birds.

Inspiration for Making Meaning	Materials for Making Meaning
• Book: *The Day I Became a Bird* by Ingrid Chabbert, illustrated by Raúl Nieto Guridi • Art: *Little Owl* or any selection by John Gould	• Loose parts: Feathers • Main material: White copy paper • Medium: Colored pencils and chalk pastels • Tools: Magnifying glasses

We Are Readers! Observe and Imagine with *The Day I Became a Bird*

We gathered outside to enjoy Ingrid Chabbert's *The Day I Became a Bird* with the chirping of the birds. We zoomed in on the illustration with ink-drawn birds by Raúl Nieto Guridi. The children were curious about the birds, and they looked closely at each feathery texture.

We Are Makers! Play and Tinker with Feathers

The following day, we gathered to feel a variety of feathers and discuss the illustration using our inferring skills. The children explained that the "birds are flying to show off their wings." They asked how they could draw birds too. We looked closely at how the artist gave the feathers texture and talked about tinkering to make this texture themselves. "We can trace,"

one child suggested. We reminded them of their background knowledge about making thin and thick lines. The children were eager to return to the art makerspace to make their own feathers.

We Are Artists! Connect and Make with John Gould

John Gould is known for his bird studies, so you can select any of his artworks to discuss feathery textures. Because of our children's interest in owls, we selected *Little Owl*. Comparing it to *The Day I Became a Bird* illustration, the children noticed the details of each drawing and determined their importance by discussing the big ideas. The children focused on the aesthetics in each image, saying the feathers made the birds pretty, and they expressed how they enjoyed the lines and patterns.

We Are ArtMakers! Share and Communicate
with Colored Pencils and Chalk Pastels

We asked, "What do you want us to know about your picture?" Here are a few of their responses as they synthesized their learning about feathery and fluffy textures by creating something new.

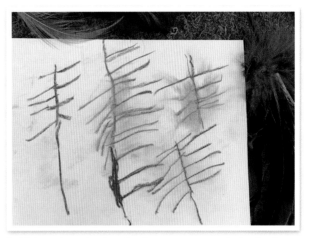

"This is a place that has feathers. Do not touch the feathers, because they are fragile." —Reed, age four

"I made feathers. They are fluffy." —Michaela, age four

ArtMaking Tip

At times throughout the investigations, you will notice that children develop a strong interest in an art element or topic. Take time to linger and follow their interest. For example, during the first reading of *The Day I Became a Bird*, the children began asking how they could use materials to become a bird. We gave them butcher paper to make their feathery and fluffy textures with combinations of lines. What a wonderful way to summarize and celebrate everything these children had learned about birds and feathery textures!

MAKING MEANING USING ORGANIC LINES TO SHOW HAIRY AND FURRY TEXTURES

Hairy and furry followed in the texture study continuum, using organic lines to draw texture. The tabletop provocation invited children to imagine making something with hairy texture by laying yarn onto playdough.

Inspiration for Making Meaning	Materials for Making Meaning
• Book: *Alma and the Beast* by Esmé Shapiro • Art: *The Peaceable Kingdom* by Edward Hicks	• Loose parts: Yarn • Main material: White copy paper • Medium: Color-changing markers (thin and thick)

We Are Readers! Observe and Imagine with *Alma and the Beast*

The children were puzzled by the mysterious place and characters during the first reading of *Alma and the Beast* by Esmé Shapiro. Later we zoomed in on a garden scene with hairy textures. They noticed "hairy butterflies," "hairy bees," "home for bees," "fountain full of stringy water flowing," and "squiggly lines."

We Are Makers! Play

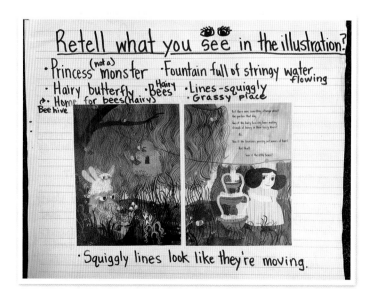

and Tinker with Yarn

The next day, we introduced tinkering with yarn to imagine where and how to add hairy texture. We posed the question, "How could you use yarn to help you make hairy texture?" and set the children loose with markers and yarn.

We Are Artists! Connect and

ArtMaking Tip

If you notice children are not as interested in the art makerspace when you bring out crayons or markers, a simple twist on a staple medium can reenergize the space. Try crayons with new shapes and wrappings or markers that can erase, change colors, or make neon or glitter shades.

Make with Edward Hicks

We introduced the children to *The Peaceable Kingdom* by Edward Hicks. Since there were so many details in this piece, we projected the image on the wall so the children could see the texture and animals. They began pointing to hairy textures and made text-to-text connections with the hairy setting and creatures like Alma.

The next day, we brainstormed a list of things that they could draw based on Alma and *The Peaceable Kingdom*. Their art was transforming from squiggly and hairy lines to settings and characters that communicated and showcased implied texture.

ArtMaking Tip

Concrete objects help children develop their vocabulary skills about texture, and then they can use this background knowledge to make implied textures in their art. Hosting animal visits is a perfect way to expand knowledge of texture. One child commented on the pig's hairy texture. Another child noticed that it looked different from Alma.

We Are ArtMakers! Share and Communicate with Color-Changing Markers

As this investigation came to a close, the children summarized and shared what they had made with the texture in their art. They synthesized their learning with their own art, full of creative places and bursting with happy and fun experiences.

"My family is outside in my garden. Grass lines and hairy trees. Ollie is a hairy dog like Alma." —Blair, age four

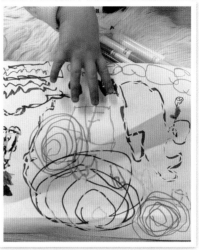

"I made a castle. All around the castle is hairy trees. The mood is happy." —Campbell Grace, age three

MAKING MEANING USING CONTOURED LINES TO SHOW SCALES

Scaly texture was next in this unit, using children's background knowledge of contoured lines. In morning meeting, the children described the mystery object as smooth and rough, which left everyone asking questions. When the sequin fabric bracelet was revealed, they all shouted, "Scales!"

Inspiration for Making Meaning	Materials for Making Meaning
• Book: *The Night Gardener* by Terry Fan and Eric Fan • Art: *Isaki and Kasago Fish* by Utagawa Hiroshige	• Loose parts: Sequins and scaled buttons • Main material: White copy paper • Medium: Crayons and watercolors • Tools: Modeling clay and sculpting tools, brushes

We Are Readers! Observe and Imagine with *The Night Gardener*

After reading *The Night Gardener*, we zoomed in on the picture of the dragon topiary because the drawing by the Fan brothers showed a strong scaly texture. The children had an aha moment when they noticed the leaves looked like scales and that the lines were like the "letter *U*" or "upside down rainbows." We added scaly texture to our texture chart.

We Are Makers! Play and Tinker with Sequins and Buttons

We returned to the illustration and discussed what the illustrators meant for us to learn. The children used their inferring skills: "The dragon was made by beautiful artists so people could be happy and have something pretty to look at." We showed them how to draw a shape, tinker with sequins or scaled buttons to imagine what the texture would look like, and then add the U-shaped lines to represent the implied texture. Since children had used many art mediums, they were able to follow multistep directions to add watercolor on top of crayon.

We Are Artists! Connect and Make with Utagawa Hiroshige

We introduced the children to *Isaki and Kasago Fish* by Utagawa Hiroshige. Hiroshige was one of the last great masters of the Japanese color woodblock prints called *ukiyo-e*. The children made text-to-text connections and determined that Hiroshige's art and the book illustration both had animals and scales—and that they could draw scales too!

We Are ArtMakers! Share and Communicate with Crayons and Watercolors

We summarized our learning by returning to our texture chart and filling in how to make the scaly texture. Students synthesized learning how to add to their character's appearance and shared how they incorporated scales into their art.

"A close-up of a mermaid's tail. They only come out when people are not looking at the ocean." —Madelyn, age four

"A great white shark. They are a type of fish." —Henry, age five

MAKING MEANING USING CIRCLES AND DOTS TO SHOW BUMPY TEXTURES

Bumpy texture was next, and so we returned to circles, ovals, and dots. The mystery box had become a special ritual children looked forward to each morning. During this investigation, they felt a bumpy rock and bubble wrap to inspire different ways to make this texture.

Inspiration for Making Meaning	Materials for Making Meaning
• Book: *The Girl and the Dinosaur* by Hollie Hughes, illustrated by Sarah Massini • Art: *Café Terrace at Night* by Vincent van Gogh	• Loose parts: Bubble wrap, bumpy rocks and pebbles • Main material: White paper • Medium: Paint • Tools: Small and thin brushes, cups for water

We Are Readers! Observe and Imagine with *The Girl and the Dinosaur*

After reading *The Girl and the Dinosaur*, we zoomed in on the picture of the dinosaur fossil magically transformed into a real dinosaur. We chose this illustration because of the circles drawn on the skin. The children commented on the spots on the dinosaur and agreed to label this as "bumpy" texture.

We Are Makers! Play and Tinker with Bubble Wrap and Rocks

When we returned to the illustration, the children noticed the bones were transforming into bumpy skin. "The dinosaur is coming alive," they inferred. We showed the children bumpy rocks and squares of bubble wrap in the makerspace. We simply asked, "What bumpy textures can you imagine making with these materials?" By now the children knew the routine of tinkering first, and they saw how it helped them imagine before making the marks on their paper. They painted the rocks and bubble wrap, squished the wrap onto the paper to see what circles it made, and dipped their fingertips in the paint to make dots.

We Are Artists! Connect and Make with Vincent van Gogh

When we showed the children a new painting from Vincent van Gogh, they noticed the bumpy texture right away and made other text-to-text connections to *The Girl and the Dinosaur*. *Café Terrace at Night* depicts an ordinary place, a restaurant van Gogh frequented. He often painted

scenes from his daily life, and we discussed with the children that they could paint anything in their world or in their imaginations. The children were eager to explore the new poster paints and fill their blank pages with bumpy textures and magical places. They used different techniques to achieve their bumpy texture: pressing the small brushes to make dots, smashing bubble wrap, and making small circle movements with the brushes.

We Are ArtMakers! Share and Communicate with Paint

The children detailed the scenes from their lives and summarized their learning about bumpy textures. We made a documentation panel to celebrate and share their learning, including bubble wrap, photos, and artworks.

"The Easter Bunny is busy at night. He leaves bumpy footprints behind while we are sleeping." —Cai, age four

"I made the house from the van Gogh painting. The ground is bumpy. This is a place where you can be happy." —Campbell Grace, age three

"I used rectangles and squares to make an anthill. All the ants together look bumpy." —Bowman, age four

ArtMaking Tip

Another method of summarizing the children's learning at the end is to document their learning throughout each phase of the ArtMaking inquiry cycle (observe and image, tinker and play, connect and make, share and communicate).

MAKING MEANING USING SQUARES AND RECTANGLES TO SHOW ROUGH TEXTURES

We introduced the children to rough textures, reviewing their knowledge of squares and rectangles. To give children more experiences with the new texture, we covered some of their blocks with sandpaper. These new materials activated their background knowledge, and they began making walls, buildings, and houses.

Inspiration for Making Meaning	Materials for Making Meaning
• Book: *The Wall in the Middle of This Book* by Jon Agee • Art: *Paris Street; Rainy Day* by Gustave Caillebotte	• Loose parts: Miniature blocks, sandpaper on wooden blocks • Main material: White construction paper • Medium: Watercolor brush markers and thin black markers

We Are Readers! Observe and Imagine with *The Wall in the Middle of This Book*

The Wall in the Middle of This Book became an instant favorite with the children. We chose this book with illustrations by Jon Agee because of the repetition of the brick wall. We zoomed in on the book illustration highlighting the brick wall, and the children used their background knowledge and the mystery box full of miniature brick blocks to label the wall as "feeling hard and rough."

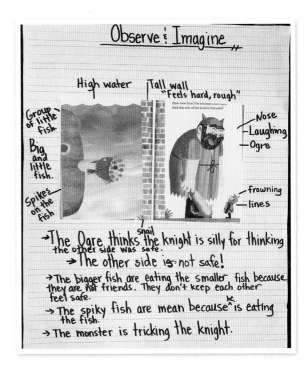

We Are Makers! Play and Tinker with Bricks and Blocks

Using their inferring skills, the children were quick to understand what was happening in the story. "The ogre thinks the knight is silly for thinking the other side was safe," they said, noticing the facial expressions of the ogre and understanding why he was laughing. They also explained that "the other side is not safe," using the text evidence of the bigger fish eating the smaller fish to support their thinking. We modeled how they could tinker with the bricks and blocks by laying them across their paper or by building structures before drawing with black markers and filling in color with watercolors.

We Are Artists! Connect and Make with Gustave Caillebotte

We viewed *Paris Street; Rainy Day* by Gustave Caillebotte together and discussed how the book illustration and the painting were alike and different. Caillebotte painted city scenes of his hometown, Paris. Children made text-to-text connections that both images had water and squares that were bricks, and that both images displayed rough texture.

We Are ArtMakers! Share and Communicate with Watercolors

Together we added squares and rectangles like a brick wall pattern to the texture chart. Here are some samples of the children's work using rough texture to communicate their own personal meaning.

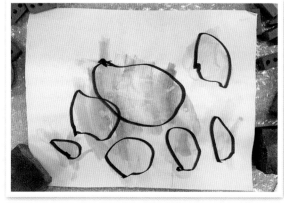

"This is my stack of bricks. It feels hard." —Shane, age three

"This is a rainbow box with bumpy and rough homes." —Madelyn, age four

MAKING MEANING USING TRIANGLES TO SHOW SHARP TEXTURES

Triangle shapes followed squares and rectangles in our shape continuum, and now we used them to imply sharp textures. To launch this investigation, we included shark teeth and arrowheads in the mystery bag. The children used new vocabulary: "ouchy," "pokey," "sharp," "spiky," "pointy," "smooth," and "felt like a triangle."

Inspiration for Making Meaning	Materials for Making Meaning
• Book: *Chalk* by Bill Thomson • Art: *Design for a Kiosk* by Alexandr Rodchenko	• Loose parts: Arrowheads and shark teeth • Main material: White copy paper • Medium: Chalk crayons and chalk pastels

We Are Readers! Observe and Imagine with *Chalk*

The wordless picture book *Chalk* by Bill Thomson features a bumpy-textured dinosaur. There are great details of teeth and nails, using triangular shapes to imply sharp textures.

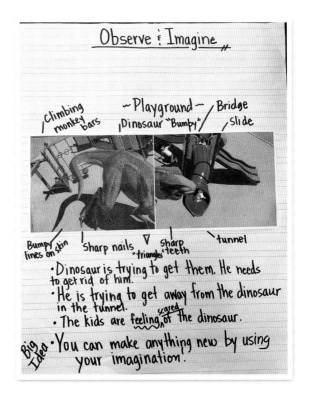

We Are Makers! Play and Tinker with Arrowheads and Shark Teeth

When we returned to the illustration to think more deeply about it, the children focused on how the dinosaur was trying to get them. Our discussion turned to how they were feeling: scared of the dinosaur. When we asked, "What do you think the illustrator wants us to know from his

picture?" they began inferring that the dinosaur was not real and only in their imaginations. That led us to state the big idea: "You can make anything new by using your imagination."

We Are Artists! Connect and Make with Alexandr Rodchenko

We showed the children *Design for a Kiosk* by Alexandr Rodchenko. They loved trying to count the triangles. They noticed that all the triangles looked sharp but were used together to create windows, doors, and even a person. We brainstormed a list to spark new ideas that they could make with triangles.

We Are ArtMakers! Share and Communicate with Chalk Crayons and Pastels

We added "jagged triangle" to our texture chart. We asked, "What did you make from your imagination that you would like to share?" The children synthesized ways to use sharp textures to add details.

"I made a dinosaur pet with my imagination. She has sharp horns. My dinosaur likes to play outside with his honey." —Fleur, age four

"This is a sun and sharp, pointy mountains. There is a pink elephant that lives in the mountains that I used with my imagination." —Michaela, age four

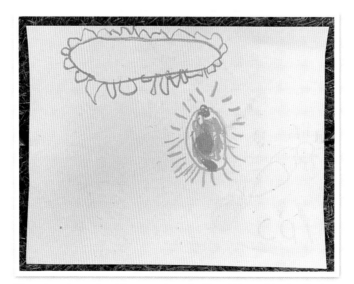

"I made a sharp cloud from my imagination. It has a blaster that shoots out suns, and it makes me happy because I made it." —Cai, age four

SYNTHESIZING OUR LEARNING ABOUT TEXTURES

We enjoyed *Where the Wild Things Are* by Maurice Sendak, then projected a large illustration from the book and invited the children to use our texture chart to help them label the textures they noticed on the creatures and plants. The class transformed the learning space into a jungle scene bursting with textures.

First the children decided what color they wanted for the background of their collaborative mural. They studied the blue sky and the texture of the illustration. The children took turns adding blue layers on the canvas and creating textures with the brushes.

To summarize our learning, we found nature loose parts to inspire the "wild place" art, and we labeled them with our texture signs. We flooded the tables with plants and flowers and invited children to use oil pastels to draw large versions of the plants on our canvas.

We then introduced children to Henri Rousseau, whose *Surprised!* inspired them to turn their wild place into a jungle. After watching videos from *Art with Mati and Dada*, gathering information and collage ideas from the National Gallery of Art, and listening to the book *The Fantastic Jungles of Henri Rousseau*, they learned that he went to botanical gardens for inspiration—coincidentally the same gardens shown in *Florette*, the book from our smooth-texture study.

After spending a week observing, studying, and drawing plants, we gathered to discuss what we needed to add to our mural. The children referred to the Rousseau paintings and expressed that they needed to include animals. Then they asked questions about how they would make these detailed drawings.

The following day, we gathered photographs of animals they wanted to include. We demonstrated how they could trace the animals using the light box, then use the photographs to choose which oil pastel colors to use. We also reminded them to recall their knowledge of lines and shapes and combine them to make the animals.

When we had compiled a nice selection of children's cutout artworks of plants and animals, we passed around a basket so children could select and place them on the canvas. They decided to start with the plants and then tuck in the animals at the end.

In the end, it was a beautiful representation of all they had learned as ArtMakers, highlighting their deep knowledge of making textures and creating meaningful art.

"These are the pink flowers spaced out in my jungle. It makes the place full of color and beauty." Spaces give children opportunities to increase their visual and comprehension skills as they use their new knowledge to create beauty.

Chapter 6

Making Meaning with Spaces

The element of space includes the size and placement of objects in a work of art. Knowledge about spaces adds complexity to our young artists' renderings and thinking. As Pelo explains, the element of space "calls forward understandings of spatial relationships and physics, perspective and proportion" (2017, 3). Because some of the concepts associated with the art element of spaces are abstract (distance, perspective), we have saved this element for the end of the year. Although the investigation into spaces is more complex than previous units, you should still consider including this unit in your ArtMaking calendar, as we have observed that harder concepts stimulate young children's curiosity and wonder. Even though the children may not have a full understanding of all the concepts (for example, horizon line), this serves as a preview for future learning and introduces new vocabulary to increase their receptive and productive languages (Lopatovska et al. 2018). Once they begin to learn about spaces, children are empowered to apply previous lessons as they intentionally think about arranging objects and ideas using colors, lines, shapes, and textures to represent their thinking more accurately.

Although in previous chapters we deconstructed artworks based on one element, we now put the pieces together and consider all aspects holistically. The children learn to use spaces and make intentional decisions using colors, lines, shapes, and textures to fill the page (foreground, background), add dimension (above and below the horizon line), and use size to show importance (big idea) and distance (perspective). Children add positional words to their vocabulary as they investigate spaces, and exploring spaces provides opportunities to master mathematical concepts, including directionality (top, bottom, up, down), order (first, second), and position (within, around, between, above, below). Additionally, some spatial concepts (crowded, full, sparse, empty, overlap) also describe the moods, settings, and other facets that add meaning to artworks (Feeney and Moravcik 1987).

Like the other ArtMaking studies, the space study begins with an inquiry that serves as an informal preassessment. We investigate what the children already know about spaces, we play with arranging items by size, we tinker with placements of objects on paper, and we figure out how we can grow their ArtMaking knowledge. Once we've gathered information on what the children already know, what they need to know, and what they are curious about, we begin our formal exploration and investigation into spaces in accordance with the continuum, moving from simple to more complex explorations of space.

We first introduce positive space (shapes or forms) and negative space (empty space between the shapes or forms). This vocabulary helps our young learners articulate where and why they place objects in their artworks, attending also to why they left some spaces blank. Next we show

A Continuum of Spaces								
Setting the Stage	Positive and Negative Spaces	Size to Determine Importance	Foreground and Background	Horizon Line	Fill the Page	Size to Determine Distance	Placement to Determine Distance	Overlapping

Setting the Stage

Positive and Negative Spaces

Size to Determine Importance

Foreground and Background

Horizon Line

Fill the Page

Size to Determine Distance

Placement to Determine Distance

Overlapping

our children how to use size to show importance or create a big idea in their art. This work reinforces lessons about measurement, comparing sizes, and labeling items according to their size (big, bigger, biggest). Next we build on the idea of using size to determine the most important object. We also introduce foregrounds and backgrounds, as items in the foreground appear larger and look closer. After this, we model how artists create depth and perspective in their foregrounds and backgrounds using a horizon line. We refer to objects above and below the horizon, introducing these new vocabulary and math concepts. We encourage the children to fill the page over time, adding details and elaborating on the meaning of their art. Moving toward complexity, we introduce the abstract concept of perspective, using size and placement to show distance. The children practice sorting concrete objects by size, comparing sizes, and placing bigger items toward the bottom of the page (to show they're close) and smaller items at the top of the page (to show they're far away). Finally, children tinker with the concept of overlap as they play with loose parts to show how items in front can block items in back. Children apply all the lessons learned thus far from colors, lines, shapes, and textures to create works of art with spaces that more accurately convey their thinking and communicate their ideas.

MAKING MEANING WITH AN INFORMAL PREASSESSMENT

After our unit on texture and making our own jungle, we repurposed the plants by spacing them out in the small world makerspace. We wanted children to notice the difference between the lush and packed jungles and the open space in their forest-inspired small world makerspace. They were learning to use the element of space to place concrete objects and translate their understanding onto paper.

During the first read of *A Forest* by Marc Martin, the children discussed what happened in the plot and commented on the aesthetics of the illustrations. "The forest is filled with all shades of green." "I like the wavy lines on the blue water." They made text-to-self connections to what they had experienced, such as "We go on hikes in our forest. It has lots of trees too" and "The plants are growing outside, just like the new forest." To immerse the children in the element of space, we invited them to notice how things are placed on the page. Are they close together, far apart, big, small? As the children wondered about these ideas, they began exploring with crayons and watercolors.

Use this QR code or type www.redleafpress.org/amk/6-t.pdf into your browser to view the chart online, or find the chart in the appendix on page 166.

We Are Readers! Observe and Imagine Using *A Forest*

The children loved the illustrations in *A Forest* that conveyed "trees are far apart." We chose this book because Martin represents several of the space concepts we would study throughout the unit. On the first selected page, we zoomed in to retell events and notice details in the picture. First they said they saw "a lot of trees." Then when we asked them to use the positional words "far apart" or "close together," they added that all the trees were far apart from one another. The second illustration represented how artists can fill a page. The children used their retelling skills to recognize the cloudy sky, grass, and buildings. I asked them to look for any blank space on the page, and they responded that there was "color everywhere on the page." In the final illustration, the children noticed the waves sweeping the buildings away. When I asked them to describe what was big and what was small, they said, "The waves are the biggest thing on the page." We invited them to observe the plants in the small world makerspace, move them around, and then draw anything from their imagination, using the inspiration from our book and discussion.

We Are Makers! Play and Tinker with Open-Ended Materials Sorted by Size, Placement, and Perspective

The following day, we gathered around a sparse-looking small world makerspace. I explained that we would create our own forest together by listening to some important words that would tell us where to place the plants and other loose parts in the makerspace. The first challenge was to place a plant far away from another plant. Children took turns and coached one another to place a plant where it wasn't touching another plant (positive and negative space). Next a child was asked to take rocks and fill the entire mirror circle to create rocky space in our forest (fill the space). The final invitation

was to place the biggest flower in front of all the other plants (size to determine importance). Children were invited to place themselves close to and far away from the forest to draw what they saw.

We Are Artists! Connect and Make with Wassily Kandinsky

Later that day, we gathered to study *Murnau: Houses in the Obermarkt* by Wassily Kandinsky. Similar to van Gogh and other artists we've studied, Kandinsky painted everyday things, like streets, neighborhoods, and inns. Recognizing beauty in ordinary and everyday places and items is a gift that comes with the development of aesthetic sensibilities. The children first made text-to-text connections between Kandinsky's artwork and Martin's illustrations, noting that they used trees and buildings to represent setting details. The children remembered how one of the illustrations filled the space and commented on how this painting had color in the sky and everywhere. They appreciated the variety of colors, sharing that they loved how both cities were

colorful. We then asked them each to select a spot in our forest and to look closely at the size and the space used. They used crayons first to draw what they saw by looking standing and looking overhead, lying beside, and sitting far away. Then they added watercolor paint on top to bring their love of color to their page and create what they observed and imagined.

We Are ArtMakers! Share and Communicate with Crayons and Watercolors

For closing circle that day, we displayed all the artwork, along with photo documentation of children tinkering in our forest, to help them summarize and reflect on what they had noticed and learned. It was amazing to notice how the children who were sitting close made close-up drawings. For example, the child on the left was sitting directly in front of the tiger, so he drew the body with black stripes and bold orange color to show it was the most important thing he saw. However, the child on the right was sitting far away at a table and drew all the plants spaced from a distance.

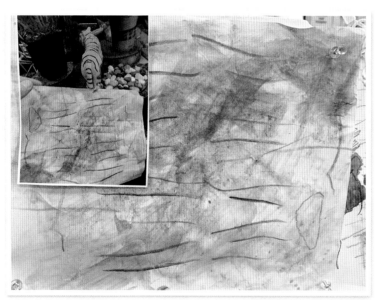

Joshua, age four, sat close to the forest and focused on the back of the tiger. He shares that he drew his tail and the water beside him by adding the black stripes with crayon and blue and orange paint on top.

Campbell Grace, age three, sat farther away from the forest. She saw all the brightly colored flowers and spaced them out across her page to represent her perspective and what she thought was beautiful.

MAKING MEANING WITH POSITIVE AND NEGATIVE SPACES

Our first investigation was about types of space. The children learn the concepts of positive space (the object on the page) and negative space (the empty space between the shapes or forms), increasing their understanding of how to place objects close together, far apart, beside, and next to one another. The children explored a sculpture makerspace, imagining how to make shapes and spaces with playdough.

Inspiration for Making Meaning	Materials for Making Meaning
• Book: *The Golden Glow* by Benjamin Flouw • Art: *Les Jeunes Amours* by René Magritte	• Loose parts: Iron filings and magnetic wands, wooden loose parts • Main material: White copy paper • Medium: Crayons and markers

We Are Readers! Observe and Imagine with *The Golden Glow*

The Golden Glow tells of a fox's journey to find the golden glow, a rare and beautiful flower. We zoomed in on two illustrations by Benjamin Flouw that featured strong examples of negative space between trees and flowers. The children used their retelling skills to label the trees and types of flowers they remembered. They noticed how the first picture was bright blue and the second illustration was dark, so we discussed how the pictures might represent day and night. We invited the children to make shapes and spaces, offering new crayons and markers to revitalize these mediums.

We Are Makers! Play and Tinker with Iron Filings and Loose Parts

We returned to the illustrations, and the children inferred that they displayed nature spaced far apart. We lingered in this stage for a few days to tinker with seeing and making space between shapes. The first loose parts that excited the children were iron fillings and magnets. The children used the magnets to move the iron filings around, seeing how space could change and move as they wished.

ArtMaking Tip

If children need a more concrete way to visualize adding space between components of their artwork, we suggest providing other loose parts. For example, the following day, we modeled placing wooden loose parts "not touching" to demonstrate another way to add space.

We Are Artists! Connect and Make with René Magritte

When we introduced the children to *Les Jeunes Amours, 1963* by René Magritte they immediately made the text-to-text connection that the objects in Magritte's art and Flouw's illustration were all far apart. Magritte's art puts commonplace things in unfamiliar scenes. The children made connections that the objects were living things in nature and that they needed space to grow. They also noticed that all these things could come from a forest. They continued to use the crayons and markers with their new inspiration, spacing things far apart to represent their ideas.

We Are ArtMakers! Share and Communicate with Crayons and Markers

We returned to our chart to summarize everything we learned about making objects close together and far apart. The children synthesized their understanding that they could draw things far apart (negative space) to call attention to the objects and places (positive space) they were making in their art.

"It's fairy world. It's a magical place." —Madelyn, age four

"I made one leaf inside a forest. It is a place to play and explore in nature." —Blair, age four

MAKING MEANING WITH SIZE AND IMPORTANCE

Next we concentrated on identifying the most important object in an image by size. This builds children's ability to identify the main idea when reading a text, while also growing their mathematical vocabulary (big, bigger, biggest, large, larger, largest). We projected large images of a flower from our picture book selection and set up a table provocation of sunflowers. We invited children to draw the biggest flowers on the table and explore geoboards to make an image. These experiences built their background knowledge in selecting one important thing and creating it across multiple mediums.

Inspiration for Making Meaning	Materials for Making Meaning
• Book: *The Little Gardener* by Emily Hughes • Art: *Le Tournesol (The Sunflower)* by Edward Steichen	• Loose parts: Flowers, wooden cookies • Main material: Paper • Medium: Oil pastels and neon watercolors • Tools: Small brushes

We Are Readers! Observe and Imagine with *The Little Gardener*

When we zoomed in on two of the selected images from *The Little Gardener* by Emily Hughes, the children noticed the huge orange flower first. These pictures are a strong example of using size to convey the main idea. The children retold how hands were touching the flower and how they saw a little boy gardener. The children then explored the loose parts, oil pastels, and watercolors to make art based on our experience with different sizes.

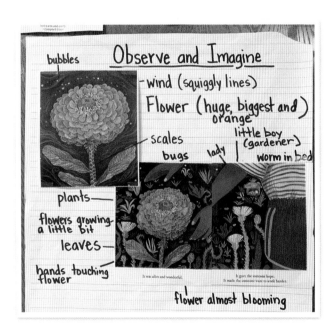

Going Deeper with ArtMaking

Use this QR code or type www.redleafpress.org/amk/6-1.pdf into your browser to Go Deeper.

We Are Makers! Play and Tinker with Geoboards and Flowers

When we discussed the illustrations the following day, the children inferred that the hands meant that someone would help the flower. They elaborated, "We will have hope that more will grow." We also set out small, medium, and large flowers and wooden cookies for tracing, to support tinkering with size.

Going Deeper with ArtMaking

Use this QR code or type www.redleafpress.org/amk/6-2.pdf into your browser to Go Deeper.

We Are Artists! Connect and Make with Edward Steichen

We showed the children *Le Tournesol (The Sunflower)* by Edward Steichen. The children made text-to-text connections that Steichen's art and Hughes's illustration both show a big, brightly colored flower made out of shapes—organic shapes in the picture book and geometric shapes in the art. Then children made their own important objects using oil pastels and watercolors.

We Are ArtMakers! Share and Communicate
with Oil Pastels and Watercolors

The children summarized that we can find the main idea by searching for the biggest thing on the page. They synthesized their learning about how they could communicate the most important thing in their own art by drawing it bigger than anything else.

"This is a forest with fish. The water is the most important thing because fish and plants need water." —Blair, age four

"It's me! I'm the biggest in the picture because everyone would love me!" —August, age three

"I made my house. The most important and biggest thing is the bed because everyone can fit in it. It will make you feel warm and comfy." —Campbell Grace, age three

MAKING MEANING WITH FOREGROUND AND BACKGROUND

In the next investigation, we identified the foreground and background in illustrations and art. These concepts build on the children's understanding of what is important in art but also gives clues about understanding an artwork's setting. The children grew their mathematical vocabulary for placement (in front of, behind). The children made characters with magnetic blocks in the table-top provocation, and we projected a landscape photograph behind them. We took photographs throughout the week to stimulate new ideas for tinkering, making, and sharing their art.

Inspiration for Making Meaning	Materials for Making Meaning
• Book: *A Stone Sat Still* by Brendan Wenzel • Art: *Mona Lisa* by Leonardo da Vinci	• Loose parts: Patterned paper, gems, nature parts, pipe cleaners, fabric pieces, magnetic blocks • Main material: White copy paper • Medium: Flair pens and tempera paint cakes • Tools: Brushes

We Are Readers! Observe and Imagine with *A Stone Sat Still*

When we zoomed in on the illustration in *A Stone Sat Still* by Brendan Wenzel, the children were drawn to the characters in the four scenes on the two-page spread. We chose this illustration because of the characters placed in the front (foreground) and the details of the setting behind (background). We also appreciated the variety of animals, colors, and hints of different seasons that would support children in imagining many possibilities for their own art instead of copying one example. The children used their

inferring skills to label each animal and describe details they noticed from the background. After the focus lesson, the children chose fabric samples for their background and then arranged loose parts to emphasize the most important object or idea.

We Are Makers! Play and Tinker with Patterned Fabric and Paper with a Variety of Loose Parts

When we returned to the illustration, children used visual text evidence to infer the places each animal inhabited: "The frog is in the forest because I see a green tree." They first tinkered in the construction makerspace to help support them making a character in the foreground that they could place on a selected background. We then gave the children photographs

of their creations from the construction makerspace for inspiration as they selected backgrounds and then made characters. Some children used their documentation to remake characters while others assembled new ideas.

We Are Artists! Connect and Make with Leonardo da Vinci

We introduced the children to the *Mona Lisa* by Leonardo da Vinci. Da Vinci was a painter, sculptor, architect, inventor, and more . . . an ArtMaker! The children were curious about the place behind the mysterious woman, and they wondered about her story. Who was she? Where was she? They were excited to learn that the *Mona Lisa* is a mystery! They made text-to-text connections between the *Mona Lisa* and Wenzel's illustration, noting that the images all had backgrounds that showed a place and then had characters, or big ideas, in front. Some children imagined new animals while others remade their characters from before.

We Are ArtMakers! Share and Communicate with Flair Pens and Tempera Paint Cakes

The children summarized that they could make a full scene like a page from a picture book. They synthesized they could do this by creating a large object in front (character, big idea) and setting details of the place in the background.

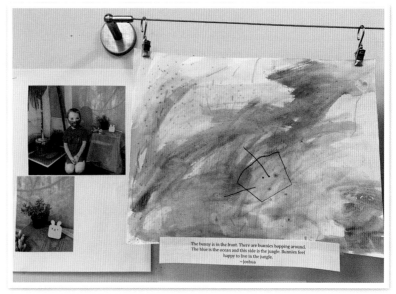

"The bunny is in the front. There are bunnies hopping around. The blue is the ocean and this side is the jungle. Bunnies feel happy to live in the jungle."
—Joshua, age four

"The giraffe is in the front. He is at the beach. It is cool so he can swim around in the water." —Reed, age four (top) "The elephant is in the front. He is in the jungle. He is drinking water from his nose and splashing it all around." —Fleur, age four (bottom)

MAKING MEANING WITH THE HORIZON LINE

We set out new tools (rulers, pencils) in a tabletop provocation to invite children to make the horizon, building on their background knowledge of how to draw horizontal lines and deciding where to place them. This investigation continued to broaden children's positional vocabulary (above, below, under, over, high, low, near, far, middle) and mathematical concepts (more, less).

Inspiration for Making Meaning	Materials for Making Meaning
• Book: *Up in the Garden and Down in the Dirt* by Kate Messner, illustrated by Christopher Silas Neal • Art: *Wheatfields Under Thunderclouds* by Vincent van Gogh	• Loose parts: Rectangular felt pieces, washi tape • Main material: White fingerpaint paper • Medium: Fingerpaint • Tools: Rulers, pencils

We Are Readers! Observe and Imagine with *Up in the Garden and Down in the Dirt*

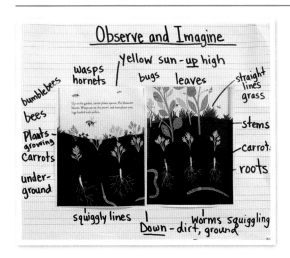

During our read aloud of *Up in the Garden and Down in the Dirt* by Kate Messner, we zoomed in on the Christopher Silas Neal illustration that showed a clear designation between the sky and the ground. This helped develop children's understanding of above, below, under, up, and down. The children used their retelling skills and

shared that the plants were growing underground, noticing the roots below the horizon line and the sun and insects flying in the sky above it. They next explored fingerpaint, moving the medium in horizontal lines to show what was up and down in their art.

We Are Makers! Play and Tinker with Rectangular Felt Pieces and Washi Tape

The children inferred that nature lives up in the sky and down in the dirt. They tinkered with felt pieces and Monet-inspired washi tape on their paper, showing a greater or lesser proportion of land and sky before tinkering with fingerpaint.

We Are Artists! Connect and Make with Vincent van Gogh

We returned to van Gogh, as he used a horizon line to separate the sky and ground in his landscape paintings. A horizon line is essential in art because it allows you to control the height of viewers' eyes as they look at the picture. Van Gogh's landscapes are a celebration of nature and ordinary people and places. The children made text-to-text connections between van Gogh's art and Neal's illustration, identifying the sky and sun above the horizon line and the ground below it. They made strong horizon lines across their pages to clearly mark the land and sky.

ArtMaking Tip

Children who need support in making a horizon line can create one with washi tape and then paint over it. When the tape is removed, this leaves a separation of the sky and the ground. (If using fingerpaint paper, beware of using other types of tape that are likely to rip the paper when removed.)

We Are ArtMakers!
Share and Communicate
with Fingerpaints

We gathered the paintings and created a display together. The students summarized by sharing that they could draw horizontal lines to make details above and below the horizon. They synthesized their understanding of more, less, above, and below.

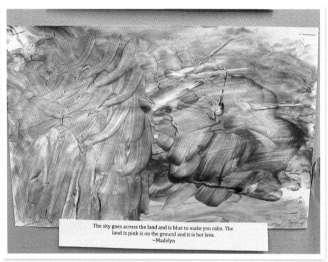

The sky goes across the land and is blue to make you calm. The land is pink is on the ground and it is hot lava.
~Madelyn

"The sky goes across the land and is blue to make you calm. The land is pink on the ground and it is hot lava." —Madelyn, age four

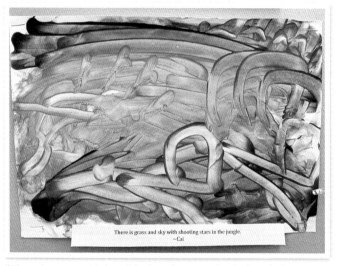

There is grass and sky with shooting stars in the jungle.
~Cai

"There is grass and sky with shooting stars in the jungle." —Cai, age four

MAKING MEANING BY
FILLING THE PAGE

We placed mirror tiles in the tabletop provocation with a variety of plastic loose parts (buttons, bottle caps, bingo chips). We asked the question, "What can you imagine making by filling up the entire mirror?" Understanding how artists fill the page builds the concept of elaboration and connects with how artists gradually add more and more details to their artwork in order to clarify their meaning.

Inspiration for Making Meaning	Materials for Making Meaning
• Book: *Packs: Strength in Numbers* by Hannah Salyer • Art: *Man on a Bench* by Horace Pippin	• Loose parts: Mirror tiles and playdough, plastic loose parts (bingo chips, bottle caps, buttons) • Main material: White copy paper • Medium: Chalk crayons, chalk pastels

We Are Readers! Observe and Imagine with *Packs: Strength in Numbers*

When zooming in on an illustration in *Packs: Strength in Numbers* by Hannah Salyer, the children noticed a lot of details. Salyer provides a strong example of filling the page. The children used their retelling skills to describe shapes, lily pads, green grass, and the number of frogs, discovering that a group of frogs is called an army. They used chalk crayons and pastels to add colors to entire pages of white paper.

We Are Makers! Play and Tinker with Mirror Tiles and Playdough

When we returned to the frog illustration, children used their inferring skills to think about the message they felt: "Sometimes we need to stop, rest, and be calm." We modeled spreading playdough to cover a mirror tile base and adding plastic loose parts on top. The children began to tinker, then referred to the details in their playdough sculpture as they took their ideas to paper.

We Are Artists! Connect and Make with Horace Pippin

We introduced children to *Man on a Bench* by Horace Pippin, a self-taught American artist who served in World War I and turned to painting to help his physical and mental recovery. He was known for expressing his experiences and memories in powerful images. In *Man on a Bench*, he filled the page with details of the setting. The image also reinforced what we had learned about background and foreground and creating the biggest image as the main idea.

The children made text-to-text connections between the book and the art, noting that both had animals, plants, sitting characters (frogs on lily pads and man on bench), and color everywhere. They used visual text evidence to explain how it was important to fill the page with color. The children then returned to the art makerspace to fill their own pages with color, including background (settings) and foreground (characters, objects) details.

We Are ArtMakers! Share and Communicate with Chalk Crayons and Chalk Pastels

When we gathered to view our art, the children summarized how they could fill the page with color to communicate. They synthesized their understanding of elaboration by filling the page.

"I made a forest that is pink, purple, and blue. This forest is colorful. There is so much pink to see!"
—Blair, age four

"This is a storm. The storm is blowing the people away."
—Cai, age four

MAKING MEANING WITH PERSPECTIVE USING SIZE

We transformed the small world makerspace with water habitats to make connections to our upcoming books. We designed this provocation with different sized rocks, shells, and blue gems for children to explore placing them in the space. The next investigation considered how artists use size to determine distance and communicate how an object is farther away if drawn small and closer when drawn bigger. This concept developed the children's mathematical skill of sorting by size and taught positional words for placing objects far and close.

Inspiration for Making Meaning	Materials for Making Meaning
• Book: *Triangle* (Shape Trilogy) by Mac Barnett, illustrated by Jon Klassen, or *Whale in a Fishbowl* by Troy Howell and Richard Jones • Art: *Red Stripe with Green Background* by Felrath Hines	• Loose parts: Different sized cookie cutters, gems, and mirrors • Main material: White copy paper • Medium: Watercolor pencils and watercolors • Tools: Brushes

We Are Readers! Observe and Imagine with *Triangle*

In *Triangle* (Shape Trilogy) by Mac Barnett, we zoomed in on the Jon Klassen illustration that showed many shapes children knew in a variety of sizes, and we discussed what the children saw in the image. We chose this illustration so we could explore shapes that appeared close and farther away. We also chose to make text-to-text connections to a favorite read aloud: *Whale in a Fishbowl*, illustrated by Richard Jones. The images reinforced the concept of drawing small to make something appear far away and drawing big to make something appear close. The children used their retelling skills by counting the number of shapes, identifying their sizes, and then recalling the story of how the triangle was running away from the square. Then they went to the art makerspace to explore watercolors and cookie cutter shapes.

We Are Makers! Play and Tinker with Different Sizes of Cookie Cutters

The children noticed different shapes, but we wanted to reinforce the different sizes of similar shapes. We sorted the objects by size and placed them on the paper to demonstrate that bigger squares looked closer and smaller squares looked farther away. They went back to the art makerspace and placed different sizes of the cookie cutters and gems on their paper before creating the shapes with watercolors.

We Are Artists! Connect and Make with Felrath Hines

We introduced the children to *Red Stripe with Green Background* by Felrath Hines because it showed two sizes of shapes. Children made text-to-text connections by noticing that Hines's art and Klassen's illustration both had shapes with big and small sizes. Inferring movement and mood, the students explained that the square in the art was jumping and having fun, whereas the shapes in the book were running and angry.

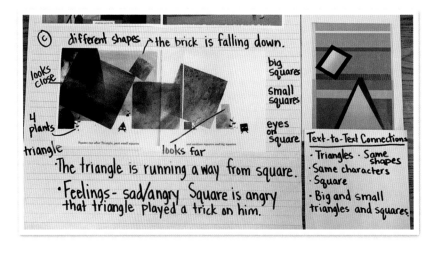

We Are ArtMakers! Share and Communicate with Watercolor Pencils and Watercolors

We summarized our learning by discussing how drawing shapes can give us confidence to make anything we wish. The children synthesized how size can give information by making details appear close and far away and can also communicate thinking, express moods, and highlight characters.

"I made cat-shaped balloons that are tied down to the ground. There is a big, medium, and small balloon. The biggest balloon is closest to us, and they want to float away." —Fleur, age four

"There is grass and hot lava. The tornado is close and is going to explode! Everyone is worried." —Cai, age four

Going Deeper with ArtMaking

Use this QR code or type www.redleafpress.org/amk/6-3.pdf into your browser to Go Deeper.

MAKING MEANING WITH OVERLAPPING

The final investigation for our space unit looked at overlapping. Overlapping happens when objects that are closer to the viewer block the view of objects behind them. This concept deepened the children's understanding of positional words (in front of, behind, on top of, underneath). It also moved children toward abstract thinking, as they began to understand that something was behind even if they could not completely see it. At a tabletop provocation, children overlapped three-dimensional shapes on the light box and stacked light-up blocks to discover how the color of one block is not visible when another block is placed on top of or beside it. This experience provided solid background knowledge for us to build on throughout this investigation.

Inspiration for Making Meaning	Materials for Making Meaning
• Book: *My Friend Earth* by Patricia MacLachlan, illustrated by Francesca Sanna • Art: *Homage to the Square* paintings by Josef Albers	• Loose parts: Light-up blocks, transparency shapes • Main material: White copy paper • Medium: Watercolor crayons • Tools: Light box, brushes, water cups

We Are Readers! Observe and Imagine with *My Friend Earth*

We read *My Friend Earth* by Patricia MacLachlan and studied the illustrations by Francesca Sanna. We chose two illustrations that gave strong examples of overlapping shapes and characters. At first, the children labeled curved lines, shapes, hills, mountains, and zebras. As our discussion continued, they began noticing groups: groups of horses, groups of mountains, and a "pack of zebras." They used their retelling skills and background knowledge to explain how the packs travel in the same direction. They also noticed that some mountains and zebras were in front of and behind one another, indicating a beginning understanding of over-

lapping. The children were invited to use shapes and light-up blocks in the art makerspace and explore making overlapping groups with these materials.

We Are Makers! Play and Tinker with Light-Up Blocks and Shapes

The following day, we revisited the illustrations to infer deeper meanings. The children went back to their idea of seeing groups. They explained that groups "help us to stay healthy and not lonely" and that they "make us feel safe, just as Mother Earth was taking care of others." We modeled a few ways to play and tinker before they took their ideas to paper. When they layered circles on top of one another on the light box, they made connections to the mountains in the picture book. One child shared that the smaller block placed in front of the larger block looked like a turtle.

We Are Artists! Connect and Make with Josef Albers

To increase the rigor of children's thinking and visual literacy skills, we presented an opportunity to make text-to-text connections across books, digital information, and art. Following the children's lead as they noticed "groups" in the illustrations, we watched documentaries on why schools of fish and other groups of animals move together. We then introduced them to *Homage to the Square* paintings by Josef Albers. Just like our ArtMakers, Albers combined the art elements: color, shapes, and spaces. The children focused on the colors and the big and small shapes and even connected back to their knowledge of how lines make shapes. Then they

explained that all the images showed groups or packs. They interpreted these "packs of squares" as Albers wanting us to enjoy the colors in nature together. They said the big idea was that "staying is love, because if we hang out together, we will feel love." Children returned to the art makerspace to make groups in their art and express these deeper messages.

We Are ArtMakers! Share and Communicate with Watercolor Crayons and Brushes

The children summarized their learning by sharing that they can make groups of characters from nature to express love, safety, and other big ideas. While discussing and sharing their artwork, they used positional words to describe where the objects were on the paper, demonstrating mastery of this mathematical vocabulary: "I drew the baby elephant in front of the mommy elephant." "The group of fish are swimming beside each other in the water." "The butterflies are flying in front of the flowers in the garden."

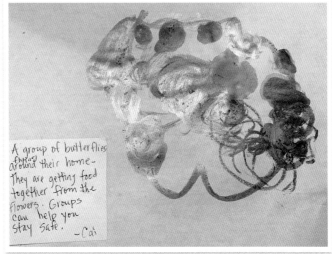

"This is a group of butterflies flying around their home. They are getting food together from the flowers. Groups can help you stay safe." —Cai, age four

"A family of elephants are playing with each other in the water. Families need to stick together so you can be safe." —Fleur, age four

"It's a heart pack that has to stay together. If one leaves, that means that the love will break. You should give love to other friends." —Madelyn, age four

SYNTHESIZING OUR LEARNING ABOUT SPACES

We gathered together during our final weeks of school and reflected on all we had learned together. Our purpose was deciding what we wanted to share with the rest of our school in a final collaborative mural, using everything we learned about the element of space. One child began by saying we learned about horizontal lines. Therefore we drew a line across the page. "We also learned that you can make things up in the sky and down." I then labeled the top "Up" and the bottom "Down." I asked the children, "What do you want to make that is up?" They discussed clouds and birds in the sky. Then a few commented that we had learned about space too. I split the upper section and wrote down their ideas about what they would see in the sky and in space. "What do you want to share about what you know about down?" They began to list all their favorite animals. A common pattern was emerging that some animals were from the gardens, jungles, and forests, while others came from the oceans. We decided to create the sky, space, jungle, and ocean to communicate all the knowledge and fun we'd had together as a class family this year.

The following day, we reviewed their thoughts from our planning chart. I asked them to remember what they knew about shades of color from our color study. We revisited illustrations from *Here We Are* by Oliver Jeffers. We zoomed in on illustrations showing the sky, space, land, and ocean, and they noticed lighter and darker colors. I handed them a handful of paint chips and asked them to explore with a partner to decide which colors they wanted in each part of our mural.

For several days, the children reflected on the colors they had selected and noticed the background colors in the picture book. They shared how to add white to make a lighter tint and black to make a darker shade. Children worked in groups to mix their own colors and create the backgrounds, reinforcing their knowledge of how to fill the space. When planning and mixing their paint for the sky, they talked about the Monet sunsets they had studied and how they loved the colors. They

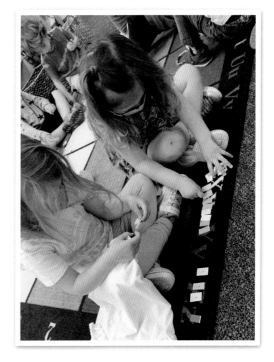

also loved the lush green jungles inspired by Rousseau and the calming shades of water they saw when Wednesday, the whale from *Whale in a Fishbowl*, finally found her true home. Since *Here We Are* represented all four spaces, it became a constant source of inspiration.

The next phase of our mural was making the foreground and adding the important details. We looked back at all the books we used throughout our studies to activate prior knowledge and inspire making, and the children then tinkered with loose parts and shapes to place their most important details on paper. Children made stars, planets, and spaceships for space. They made birds, clouds, and sunsets for the sky. Plants, jungle animals, and small worms and insects filled the land; and coral, shells, and marine life were for the ocean.

We introduced the children to *Josie's Dream* by Frederick J. Brown. Brown, like our ArtMakers, focused on aesthetics in creating as many beautiful things as he could for the world to enjoy. The children made text-to-text connections to the colorful parts of our Earth, noticing how the illustrations in *Here We Are* and Brown's art fill the space and use many details to communicate ideas seen in the sky and on the ground, in reality, and in imagination and dreams. The children then gathered their art and began arranging the details in the foreground of the mural. Mindful of the horizon line that separated the backgrounds, the children sorted the art, keeping similar pictures together and determining their importance by size and placement.

The final documentation represents their knowledge of using space to communicate details about a place. It shows the importance of using size and placement to show distance and sends a strong message about the beauty of the world and the joy they experienced while learning together this year. We encourage you to linger with their art and read their final words so you can take ArtMaking with you and draw your own conclusions: "This is our year of learning. Our world is a beautiful place. When you take the time to look, your mind will grow."

"We can make beautiful art together!" shared one child as we reflected on our powerful year of learning. "Look at all the colors and lines." "We added texture to our branches too." "We are just like illustrators!"

Conclusion

Synthesizing Our ArtMaking with Design

As the culmination of our explorations and studies, design demonstrates how art elements can be combined to communicate thinking. Design is the process or product that highlights how a child puts together colors, lines, shapes, textures, and spaces to communicate a feeling, thought, movement, idea, mood, story, and more. It showcases how a child chooses to combine, emphasize, and manipulate the elements of art to communicate their message more clearly. The designers, our ArtMakers, apply visual literacy and comprehension strategies as they produce art and communicate complex thinking.

We'd like to invite you to tour our design studio to see how we've captured learning, using ArtMaking as our framework. Capturing and framing learning represented in design can be done through documentation. Documentation requires more than a display and more than children's words, so we add interpretation and explanation as a framework to demonstrate learning. Children use many languages to express their thinking, including imagination, tinkering, and art. In the sample documentation panels below, we try to capture children's collaborative designs and languages to communicate important thinking and learning from their worlds. We hope you enjoy our ArtMaking design tour!

MAKING MEANING WITH DESIGN

Welcome to our studio of design! We're glad you toured the world of ArtMaking with us! Today we're highlighting the design that started out as a nature walk inspired by *The Tree That's Meant to Be* by Yuval Zommer, which then led to a color study based on the imaginations and observations of our young ArtMakers.

Color

The children made discoveries as they immersed their senses in nature and color. They mixed, invented, and named their greens, all while developing their aesthetic sensitivities about what constitutes beauty in their worlds.

They played and tinkered with nature loose parts, light, and shadows to cut and glue and arrange and experience what each evergreen felt like, inspired by *Pick a Pine Tree* by Patricia Toht.

They tinkered with nature loose parts to make their own tree inspired by our line study and *The Tree That's Meant to Be*. Using straight lines, curved lines, angled lines, and horizontal lines, they arranged the sticks by size and placed them from longest to shortest.

Next they designed an entire tree. After a great deal of observation, measurement, comparison, discussion, debate, and brainstorming, they decided leaves were mostly shaped like triangles. They selected cardboard triangles (isosceles, equilateral, and acute) and painted them each a unique shade of green.

Textures and Spaces

Lines and Spaces

Colors and Shapes

Colors, Shapes, and Spaces (before)

Colors, Shapes, and Spaces (after)

The children were inspired by and connected to artist Paul Klee as they made their tree, arranging the triangles base to base, large to small, and overlapping. They thoughtfully placed the dark, shaded, light, and tinted greens to make the tree aesthetically pleasing.

The children thought something was missing from their tree. They drew lines to show movement and create a peaceful mood. They connected to Monet's sunset colors and the lines throughout *Daniel's Good Day* by Micha Archer. They referred to our line chart to choose different lines.

Colors, Lines, Shapes, and Spaces

After studying, talking, and thinking about their work, they decided to add textures to the leaves. They returned to their textures chart and described the pine needles feeling "prickly" or "tickly because it tickles your skin." They then drew angled lines on the leaves to communicate what the tree felt like.

The children had created movement and a peaceful mood with the lines, but the background and foreground were not clearly delineated. They added a horizon line to make sure the tree was the big idea in their design. They filled the page by coloring the background. Finally, they decided it was finished!

Texture

The children reflected on their ArtMaking journey, making and sharing together. They each wanted a piece of their tree and asked to draw their own version of their collaborative art. One child explained, "I made a Christmas tree. It's the most important time of the year because we made the tree together as friends."

We hope this ArtMaking process inspires you to innovate new ways to enrich your literacy teaching and open up opportunities for children to communicate through art. Use your favorite books you have on hand right now and begin by noticing what you see in illustrations and art. The children will lead you the rest of the way with their ideas, interests, and artistic creations. As the educators from Reggio Emilia, Italy, remind us, "Make sure, above all, that children become familiar in their minds with images, that they know how to keep them alive, that they

Colors, Lines, Shapes, Textures, Spaces . . . Design!

learn the pleasure of reactivating them, regenerating them, and multiplying them with the maximum amount of personal and creative intervention" (Gandini et al. 2015, 12–13). We can't wait to see how you create your studio and showcase the art you create with your community of learners.

I made Christmas time. It's the most important time of the year.
~Cai

Appendix

Chapter 3: Getting Ready for ArtMaking

ArtMaking Process	Lesson Details	Art Makerspace Invitation	Making Meaning Examples
Phase 1 **We Are Readers!** Observe and Imagine	• Return to *In a Jar* by Deborah Marcero and zoom in on one illustration. • Engage the children in **retelling** the image you selected by decoding/listing everything they see. Focus children's attention on the lines.	Invite children to explore art makerspace with book inspiration, crayons, colored pencils, and markers.	Retelling: • "I see straight lines." • Hand motions in the air repeating lines they see. Teacher asks, "What should we call this?" • "That line is curved like a rainbow."
Phase 2 **We Are Makers!** Play and Tinker	• Return to illustration and remind them of what they noticed. • Engage children in **inferring** for meaning in the illustration, using text evidence to support their ideas. • Model using loose parts to **visualize** what to make.	Invite children to make with nature loose parts, crayons, and markers with the purpose of knowing how to use the materials.	Inferring: • "The red makes the place seem warm." • "I think the water is rough because all those lines."
Phase 3 **We Are Artists!** Connect and Make	• Introduce Claude Monet and make **text-to-text connections** between his painting and the illustration. • **Determine the importance** of the artist's choices (elements).	Invite children to use their nature loose parts and crayons/markers.	Text-to-text-connections: • "The wheat field and the water both look like it's moving." • "I see squiggly lines here [pointing] and on the mountains."
Phase 4 **We Are ArtMakers!** Share and Communicate	• Revisit Monet painting and highlight children's artwork. • **Summarize** what we learned about the big idea. Ask, "What do you want others to know when they look at your picture?"	Invite children to **synthesize** their understanding and use loose parts and crayons, colored pencils, or markers with the new purpose of communicating a big idea.	Summarizing: • "We can use lines instead of scribbling." • "We learned that lines can make things pretty." • "Lines help us draw more details in our pictures." Synthesizing: • "I used lines to make the letter *X*. Lines help you make letters."

Chapter 4: Getting Ready for ArtMaking

ArtMaking Process	Lesson Details	Art Makerspace Invitation	Making Meaning Examples
Phase 1 **We Are Readers!** Observe and Imagine	• Return to the book *Walter's Wonderful Web* by Tim Hopgood and zoom in on one illustration. • Engage the children in **retelling** the visual image you selected by decoding/listing everything they see. Connect to the lines they have learned and then focus children's attention on the shapes they might notice.	Invite children to fully explore art makerspace with book inspiration, crayons, flair pens, and Sharpie markers.	Retelling: • "I see a line." • "The lines are connecting." • "I see the moon." • Teacher asks, "What shape should we call this?"
Phase 2 **We Are Makers!** Play and Tinker	• Return to illustration and remind them of what they noticed. • Engage children in **inferring** the meaning of the illustration by using text evidence to support their ideas. • Model using loose parts to help them **visualize** what to make.	Invite children to make with yarn, translucent shapes, crayons, felt-tip pens, and markers to determine whether they know how to use the materials.	Inferring: • "Walter never gave up." • "His web is strong. All the lines together make it stronger."
Phase 3 **We Are Artists!** Connect and Make	• Introduce Alexander Calder and make **text-to-text connections** between what they see in the illustration and his painting (*Quilt, Untitled*). • **Determine the importance** of the artist's choices (elements).	Invite children to use their yarn, translucent shapes, and crayons/markers to communicate a big idea.	Text-to-text-connections: • "They both have strong lines." • "They both use lines and shapes to make a pretty picture." Inferring a big idea: • "He wants us to know that you can use shapes to create any picture."
Phase 4 **We Are ArtMakers!** Share and Communicate	• Revisit Calder painting and highlight the children's artwork. • **Summarize** what we learned about the big idea and mood. Ask, "What is the message you want others to know about your picture?"	Invite children to **synthesize** their understanding and make with their loose parts and crayons/markers or watercolors to communicate a big idea.	Summarizing: • "We can use shapes to create pictures, people, and animals." • "We can trace shapes if we don't know how to make them." Synthesizing a big idea: • "I used shapes to make a unicorn so people know that they do exist."

Chapter 5: Getting Ready for ArtMaking

ArtMaking Process	Lesson Details	Art Makerspace Invitation	Making Meaning Examples
Phase 1 **We Are Readers!** Observe and Imagine	• Return to the book *A Little Bit Brave* by Nicola Kinnear and zoom in on one illustration. • Engage the children in *retelling* the visual image you selected by decoding/listing everything they see. • Prompt them to make connections to texture by asking them, "What does that feel like?"	Invite children to explore the art makerspace and encourage making crayon rubbings with different objects and texture plates.	Retelling: • "I see water. It is wet and smooth." • "I see rabbits. I would feel fur and soft." • "The bird is wearing a scarf. It is fluffy." • "The bird has a soft wing."
Phase 2 **We Are Makers!** Play and Tinker	• Return to illustration and remind them of what they noticed. • Engage children in *inferring* the illustration by using text evidence to support their ideas. • Model using the loose parts to help them *visualize* what to make.	Model making crayon rubbings by placing an object under the paper and moving the flat crayon with down strokes. Prompt thinking about what place or character they could imagine this texture becoming.	Inferring: • "You should try new things."
Phase 3 **We Are Artists!** Connect and Make	• Introduce Martin Johnson Heade and make *text-to-text connections* between what they saw in the illustration and his painting. • *Determine the importance* of the choices from the artist (elements) by asking, "What is this place and what details make you think this?"	Invite children to use the textured stamps and nature objects to make crayon rubbings and add watercolors to make a setting with textured details.	Text-to-text-connections: • "They both have birds, wings, and Christmas trees in the pictures." Inferring mood: • "Their faces show that they are feeling joy."
Phase 4 **We Are ArtMakers!** Share and Communicate	• Revisit Heade painting and highlight children's artwork. • *Summarize* what we learned about the big idea and mood. Ask, "What texture do you want us to see?"	Invite children to *synthesize* their understanding and make with their loose parts and crayons/markers or watercolors to communicate with texture.	Summarizing: • "We can make texture." • "There are many different kinds of texture—soft, fluffy, spiky." Synthesizing mood: • "This is a forest where bad guys turned into a dark place. It feels dark to visit there now."

Chapter 6: Getting Ready for ArtMaking

ArtMaking Process	Lesson Details	Art Makerspace Invitation	Making Meaning Examples
Phase 1 **We Are Readers!** Observe and Imagine	• Return to *A Forest* by Marc Martin and zoom in on three illustrations. • Engage the children in **retelling** the visual image you selected by decoding/listing everything they see. • Ask questions to introduce them to concepts of space. "Are they far apart or close together?" "How did the illustrator use the space on the whole page?" "What is the biggest and smallest thing in the picture?"	Invite children to explore some of the space concepts with crayons and watercolors in the art makerspace.	Retelling: • "The trees are far apart." • "There is color everywhere on the page. No white space." • "Waves are the biggest thing on the page."
Phase 2 **We Are Makers!** Play and Tinker	• Return to the illustrations and remind them of what they noticed. • Engage children in **inferring** from the illustrations by using text evidence to support their ideas. • Prompt children to use loose parts and the images to help them **visualize** different ways to draw the same area.	Engage children in practicing using space in a concrete way. Invite them to place plants in the small world makerspace, using positional words. "Place the biggest plant in front of our forest." Invite children to stand, sit, or lie down close or far and then draw what they see to practice perspective.	Inferring: • "We should take care of the planet." • "Nature is a beautiful place."
Phase 3 **We Are Artists!** Connect and Make	• Introduce Wassily Kandinsky and make **text-to-text connections** between the illustrations and his painting *Murnau: Houses in the Obermarkt*. • **Determine the importance** of the artist's choices.	Invite children to view the living forest from different angles and communicate their new perspective of what they see.	Text-to-text-connections: • "They both have buildings and trees." • "There is color filling the sky." • "Both cities are colorful." Inferring a big idea: • "If you want beautiful cities, then you have to take care of it. Don't throw trash and make it smoky."
Phase 4 **We Are ArtMakers!** Share and Communicate	• Revisit Kandinsky painting and highlight children's artwork. • **Summarize** what we learned about the big idea. Ask, "What part of the forest did you decide to create?"	Invite children to **synthesize** their understanding and share what they have learned in this investigation.	Summarizing: • "We can draw things close up or far away to make it look little." Synthesizing: • "We can all see things differently, and it can all be beautiful."

References

Arrow, Emily. 2020. *Studio: A Place for Art to Start.* Plattsburgh, NY: Tundra.

Barbe-Gall, Françoise. 2018. *How to Talk to Children about Art.* Chicago: Chicago Review.

Brumberger, E. 2011. "Visual Literacy and the Digital Native: An Examination of the Millennial Learner." *Journal of Visual Literacy* 30 (1): 19–46.

Bryan, Trevor Andrew. 2019. *The Art of Comprehension: Exploring Visual Texts to Foster Comprehension, Conversation, and Confidence.* Portsmouth, NH: Stenhouse.

Callow, Jon. 2008. "Show Me: Principles for Assessing Students' Visual Literacy." *The Reading Teacher* 61 (8): 616–26.

Ceppi, Giulio, and Michele Zini, eds. 1998. *Children, Spaces, Relations: Metaproject for an Environment for Young Children.* Reggio Emilia, Italy: Reggio Children.

Feeney, Stephanie, and Eva Moravcik. 1987. "A Thing of Beauty: Aesthetic Development in Young Children." *Young Children* 42 (6): 7–15.

Felten, Peter. 2008. "Visual Literacy." *Change* 40 (6): 60–63.

Gandini, Lella, Lynn Hill, Louise Cadwell, and Charles Schwall, eds. 2015. *In the Spirit of the Studio: Learning from the Atelier of Reggio Emilia,* 2nd ed. New York: Teachers College.

Goldberg, Barry. 2014. "Seeing Meaning." *Art & Early Childhood: Personal Narratives & Social Practices* 31 (4): 27–36.

Harvey, Stephanie, and Anne Goudvis. 2008. *The Primary Comprehension Toolkit,* 2nd ed. Portsmouth, NH: Heinemann.

Kandinsky, Wassily. 1979. *Point and Line to Plane.* New York: Dover.

Kind, Sylvia. 2014. "Material Encounters." In "Materiality in Early Childhood Studies," edited by Laurie Kocher, Veronica Pacini-Ketchabaw, and Sylvia Kind. *International Journal of Child, Youth and Family Studies* 5 (4.2): 865–77.

Liu, Jianli, Edwin Lughofer, and Xianyi Zeng. 2015. "Aesthetic Perception of Visual Textures: A Holistic Exploration Using Texture Analysis, Psychological Experiment, and Perception Modeling." *Frontiers in Computational Neuroscience* 9 (34). www.ncbi.nlm.nih.gov/pmc/articles /PMC4631837.

Lopatovska, Irene. 2016. "Engaging Young Children in Visual Literacy Instruction." *Proceedings of the Association for Information Science and Technology* 53 (1): 1–5. https://doi.org/10.1002 /pra2.2016.14505301101.

Lopatovska, Irene, Sarah Hatoum, Saebra Waterstraut, Lisa Novak, and Sara Sheer. 2016. "Not Just a Pretty Picture: Visual Literacy Education through Art for Young Children." *Journal of Documentation* 72 (6): 1197–1227. https:doi.org/10.1108/JD-02-2016-0017.

Lopatovska, Irene, Tiffany Carcamo, Nicholas Dease, Elijah Jonas, Simen Kot, Grace Pamperien, Anthony Volpe, and Kurt Yalcin. 2018. "Not Just a Pretty Picture Part Two: Testing a Visual Literacy Program for Young Children." *Journal of Documentation* 74 (3).

Miller, Debbie. 2012. *Reading with Meaning: Teaching Comprehension in the Primary Grades,* 2nd ed. Portsmouth, ME: Stenhouse.

Nicholson, Simon. 1971. "How Not to Cheat Children—The Theory of Loose Parts." *Landscape Architecture* 62:30–34.

Oludare, Obaleye Joseph, Albert B. Adeboye, Isidore C. Ezema, and Ejiga Opaluwa. 2020. "Shapes and Aesthetic Perception: A Case Study of University of Lagos Senate Building Façade." *International Journal of Scientific & Technology Research* 9 (3): 765–69.

Pantaleo, Sylvia. 2005. "'Reading' Young Children's Visual Texts." *Early Childhood Research and Practice* 7 (1). https://ecrp.illinois.edu/v7n1/pantaleo.html.

Pelo, Ann. 2017. *The Language of Art: Inquiry-Based Studio Practices in Early Childhood Settings,* 2nd ed. St. Paul, MN: Redleaf.

Penfold, L. 2019. "Material Matters in Children's Creative Learning." *Journal of Design and Science.* https://jods.mitpress.mit.edu/pub/bwp6cysy.

Raney, Karen. 1998. "A Matter of Survival: On Being Visually Literate." *The English & Media Magazine* 39:37–42.

Reggio Children. n.d. "The Wonder of Learning: The Hundred Languages of Children." Accessed November 8, 2021. www.reggiochildren.it/en/exhibitions/the-wonder-of-learning-the-hundred-languages-of-children.

Serravallo, Jennifer. 2018. *Understanding Texts and Readers: Responsive Comprehension Instruction with Leveled Texts.* Portsmouth, NH: Heinemann.

Smithsonian American Art Museum. n.d. "Alma Thomas." Accessed November 8, 2021. https://americanart.si.edu/artist/alma-thomas-4778.

Sulzby, Elizabeth. 1994. "Children's Emergent Reading of Favorite Storybooks: A Developmental Study." In *Theoretical Models and Processes of Reading,* 4th ed., edited by R. B. Ruddell, M. R. Ruddell, and H. Singer, 244–80. Newark, DE: International Reading Association.

Thompson, Robin Chappele, and Michelle Kay Compton. 2020. *Makerspaces: Remaking Your Play and STEAM Early Learning Areas.* St. Paul, MN: Redleaf.

Vecchi, Vea. 2010a. *Art and Creativity in Reggio Emilia: Exploring the Role and Potential of Ateliers in Early Childhood Education.* New York: Routledge.

Vecchi, Vea. 2010b. "Poetics of Learning." In *In the Spirit of the Studio: Learning from the Atelier of Reggion Emilia,* edited by Lella Gandini, Lynn Hill, Louise Cadwell, and Charles Schwall, 17–21. New York: Teachers College.

Ventura, Anya. 2013. "Designing Representational Systems." MIT Center for Art, Science, & Technology, May 1, 2013. https://arts.mit.edu/designing-representational-system.

Walsh, Maureen. 2003. "'Reading' Pictures: What Do They Reveal? Young Children's Reading of Visual Texts." *Literacy* 37 (3): 123–30.

Wang, X. Christine, Keely Benson, Corinne Eggleston, and Bin Lin. 2019. "A Guided, Exploration-Based Visual Arts Program for Preschoolers." *Young Children* 74 (1): 72–80.

Wohlwend, Karen. 2008. "Play as a Literacy of Possibilities—Expanding Meanings in Practices, Materials, and Spaces." *Language Arts* 86 (2): 127–36.